How to Calm a
Challenging
Child

Miriam Chachamu
Family Therapist

Illustrations by Tomas Woodbridge

foulsham
LONDON • NEW YORK • TORONTO • SYDNEY

foulsham

Capital Point, 33 Bath Road, Slough, Berkshire,
SL1 3UF, England

Foulsham books can be found in all good bookshops and direct from
www.foulsham.com

ISBN: 978-0-572-03495-5

Copyright © 2008 Miriam Chachamu
Last reprinted 2012

Cover photograph © Superstock

A CIP record for this book is available from the British Library

The moral right of the author has been asserted

Printed in Great Britain by Martins the Printers Ltd

Contents

My thanks go to...

... my family members, who have had to put up with my evolving parenting skills (and, at times, the lack of them) for the past 20 years; Noël Janis-Norton, the originator of the Calmer, Easier, Happier parenting programme, who welcomed me to The New Learning Centre and whose wisdom inspired many of the ideas in this book; the many parents and families who came to my courses and consultations, and gave me an open and honest insight into their family life; all my friends, family, clients and colleagues who have helped me with this book – you are far too many for me to be able to name you all; my daughter Shani Chachamu for her Photoshop wizardry; my friends Denise Winn and Lea Filip for their invaluable comments on the manuscript; everyone at Foulsham who has supported me through the process of making this book a reality; and, of course, to Tomas Woodbridge, whose lively and accurate cartoons smile at you from the pages of this book.

Foreword

Every honest parent will admit that there are moments when their children drive them to distraction. Other people's children seem to go to bed without a fuss, eat the food they are given and clear up when they are asked; your own children, however, seem uniquely grumpy and unco-operative. As the children get older, the little temper tantrums that were once sweet expressions of toddler independence come to seem like symptoms of a deep malaise and the little voice inside your head that has been telling you, 'Hey, I'm the best mother that ever lived' suddenly changes tone. 'You are making a mess of this,' it says as you burst into tears.

At such moments what you need is a kindly and wise person to talk to, someone who has been through these dramas and can prod you gently into behaving a little better yourself so that your children can, in turn, learn to be calm and co-operative. I was fortunate that when I hit parenting bottom, I came across the New Learning Centre and Miriam Chachamu who was working there.

When I signed up for a course of parenting classes with Miriam, my children were aged from 11 to two. Individually I adored them, of course, but as a group all they ever seemed to do was squabble. Frazzled and over-tired from running a home and working full-time, I remember feeling pessimistically that – short of sending me on a long rest cure – there was no way she could help. Nevertheless, I decided to go to a couple of classes just in case I could learn from them. Soon I found that the weekly sessions were not only fascinating but indispensable.

In part, it was Miriam's personal blend of cheerfulness and sympathy that made a difference. She was open about admitting that she too had once feared that she was nothing like the parent she had wanted to be: memorably, she admitted to the shame of once having pushed her daughter out of bed in frustration because she wouldn't get up after numerous reminders and threats. Such fellow feeling from one who now seemed like everyone's idea of a dream cosy mummy was very reassuring.

But her group sessions gave me more than just companionship in my self-doubts. Each week the group would explore a common problem – it might be dealing with fights or managing children who wouldn't stay in their own beds – and look at ways to handle the situation better. After every class each of us had homework to do: we had to address a situation differently and see if we

achieved a different result. Week after week we had
improvements to report and our confidence grew.
  I'm very glad now that she has found the time to make her
unique brand of wisdom into a book.

Cassandra Jardine
Mother of five children, *Daily Telegraph* journalist and
author of *How to Be a Better Parent* and *Positive Not Pushy*

Introduction

Becoming a parent is one of life's most profound experiences. No matter how much you read about it, think about it or talk about it, nothing can prepare you for the intensity of feeling that most people experience when their child is born. Suddenly a tiny, helpless baby is totally dependent on you. From this point on, you will always have to balance your own wants and needs with the wants and needs of your child.

You probably started out with lots of hopes and dreams. A few years on, your family life may typically look more like this:

As your children grow up, their needs become more complex. They need your love, care, attention, time, energy, patience, knowledge and wisdom as well as some practical help with getting dressed, brushing their teeth, preparing food, doing their homework and being in the right place at the right time.

Many new parents have only distant memories of their own childhood, and not much experience of living with children. They are not sure what to expect and how to deal with the everyday challenges of raising children. Extended families are not always around, and friends are busy trying to cope themselves.

I believe that to manage the chaos effectively and meet everyone's needs, we can't just rely on love and good intentions. We need a good understanding of our children's perspective and of family dynamics, together with practical skills – skills that can be learned.

This guide is not a child-rearing manual and I do not see myself as a 'know it all' expert. However, I have worked with many families as well as having raised my own three children. The ideas and skills in this book have helped many parents to communicate better and experience more affection towards their children, reducing arguments and stress. I hope they may be useful to you too.

This book is designed for parents of children aged from about two (or whenever they understand some language) up to pre-teenage years. Much of what you read about can be effective with teenagers and adults, although you will need to adjust your language accordingly. My belief is that almost anyone who has contact with children will find new ideas and useful tips in this book, whether they are parents or not.

The practical skills covered in Part 2 focus mainly on problem areas, because this is what parents look for help with! But, of course, in every family, there is plenty that goes right. Your children may be happy to get up in the morning, eat a variety of healthy foods, or get on well with each other. Congratulate yourself on what is going right, even if, sometimes, other people think that you should do things differently. There is no single, correct way to raise children. As long as all family members are happy, and you as parents feel that your values are being upheld, you are doing fine!

What will you gain from reading this book?

- A better understanding of your children's perspective and needs. This is the first essential step towards improving your relationships and having a happier home.

- Positive communication skills to help you put this understanding into practice. You will find ideas to motivate your children to be their best – happy, confident, secure and respectful of others.

- Strategies to deal with everyday problems as they arise.

I can promise you that if you take on the ideas in this book, and put your new communication skills into practice consistently, your family life will be transformed. There will be more co-operation and less stress in your home, more laughter and fewer tears.

How to use this book

Most of us, when presented with a new idea, notice first what we do not like about it: we think of the times when it will not work for us, or about situations in which it will be impractical to use, or we question whether the idea is compatible with our culture or in line with our values. This is a common and natural human reaction to anything new. Perhaps it is even a part of the mechanism that kept us humans safe early on in our evolution – when faced with something new, we always had to make a quick risk assessment so that we could keep away from danger.

I am inviting you to read this book differently. As you read, notice any reservations that you may have, accept that these reservations help you ensure that you do not take on something that is not right for you, and then ask yourself questions such as:

- In spite of these reservations, is there any value for me in this new idea?

- Is there a way for me to adapt it so that it suits my family?

- How can I change the language in the example to suit my style and personality?

If you keep this frame of mind while reading the book I promise you will get a lot out of it.

The book is divided into two parts. The first is about understanding children and families, and contains some important principles about how we operate as human beings, and about how families and relationships function. The second part shows how these ideas translate into practical communication skills that you can use with your kids. I recommend that you read the first part first – the practical skills will make much more sense once you read the principles.

This book is a tool to use, not to preserve. I hope you will feel free to write your comments on it and use coloured or highlighter pens to mark things you like or reservations that you have, together with points for discussion with the other adults involved in raising your children. Make this book your own!

If you want your children to improve, put the parenting skills into practice. Changing your understanding and your thinking is not enough. If you want results, you need to act differently.

Changing the way you do things requires a huge effort, so do not despair at the first hurdle. Remember that the rewards are immense. Many families have gone through this process already, and I have asked some of them to share their experience with you. You will come across their stories as you read through the book (all the names have been changed).

Be sure to congratulate yourself on your progress, even if improvement to your family life is not as quick as you would like it to be. Changing old habits is often hard and it is only to be expected that you slip back into your old ways from time to time. Recognise each small step in your own progress, and be proud of it. Be kind and generous to yourself.

How long will all this take?

Most people see a noticeable change in their children's behaviour within a few days of using the positive parenting skills, some even seeing immediate improvement; other families take longer. Please try to give the skills a month of consistent use.

A month may seem like a long time, but if you think of it in the context of your life with your children, it is not much at all. And once you start seeing the results of your new insights and improved practices you will never want to look back.

www.enjoyourchildren.com

At my website, enjoyourchildren. com, you will find additional information on parenting, and you can post questions and see the answers to other parents' queries. Simply register on the site to benefit from the regular updates.

PART 1

Understanding children and families

If you have more than one child, or have spent time around babies, you will probably have noticed that babies are different from each other in temperament right from birth. Some babies are easy-going: they sleep well, eat well and are generally healthy and happy. When a child is easy, you can see this positive cycle of reinforcement most of the time:

The easy child smiles at the world and the world smiles back.

Other babies are irritable, difficult to pacify, highly sensitive to their environment and often seem to have boundless energy. I call these sorts of babies and children 'spirited' rather than difficult.* They are often lively and full of surprises and, when they are in a good mood, they are great fun to be with. But, overall, spirited children have more complex needs than easy-going children, so their parents face a bigger challenge in bringing them up.

---

* The term 'spirited children' was coined by Mary Sheedy Kurcinka (see Recommended reading, page 200).

When a child is spirited, the cycle in the early years can be a negative one that looks more like this:

Life for spirited children is hard, and they make life hard for everyone else around them.

By the time they start their education, easy-going children and spirited children have a completely different experience of life. Typically, easy-going children get approval and positive attention and feel loved and accepted, while spirited children are told off regularly, hear lots of 'no's' and 'stop it's', possibly get smacked by their exasperated parents, and are already seeing themselves as trouble.

Most children, of course, fall somewhere between these two extremes. However, there are significant numbers of spirited children around and, not surprisingly, their parents are usually the ones who read and write parenting books!

It is not your fault

If your children often misbehave and you find yourself losing your temper, being sarcastic or feeling depressed; if you sometimes hate your children or are so furious that you want to throw them out of the window or send them away for a year or two, you are in good company. Most parents, myself included, have felt similarly at times. Being a parent is extremely demanding, even when your children are easy-going. If you have a spirited child, it is even more so! We have all experienced anger and frustration with our children at times, or felt that we could not cope.

If, however, you feel frustrated more than occasionally, it is possible that you are locked into a negative cycle similar to the one illustrated on page 12. This does not mean that you have failed, or that you are a bad parent. It only means that raising your children has become a challenge, perhaps a bigger challenge than you wish. If you aim to deal with this challenge successfully you will need to develop your understanding of your child's perspective and needs, and to acquire new communication skills. Loving your child and hoping for the best may not be enough.

You can improve things right now

When children misbehave, are very clingy, or lacking in self-confidence, it may be tempting to think that it is just a phase they will grow out of. This may be right. But before they grow out of it, if they indeed do, you, your child and your whole family may experience years of unnecessary stress.

But you can use your feelings of anger and frustration, as well as your child's misbehaviour, positively – as signs that you need a rethink about how you are managing the situation. This can be your alarm system, telling you that you need to do something different. If you keep doing what you always do, you'll keep getting what you always get.

You can almost instantly improve many children's behaviour, mood and wellbeing by making sure that they eat healthily, exercise, spend enough time outdoors and sleep well. See pages 196–99 for the basics on how to do this.

But that is just part of the solution. To get a different result *you* have to do something different. Regardless of your child's inborn temperament, you are holding the keys to the solution. When you change what *you* do, they will respond to you differently and the negative cycle can transform into a positive one. This is powerful knowledge!

To be able to change what you do, you need a better understanding of how you and your children tick, and that is what this first part of the book is about.

CHAPTER 1

Getting what we all need

All living creatures, whether they are plants, insects or animals, have basic needs, and they will not thrive if these needs are not met. People and their children are no different! Understanding this is the key to learning to become a more effective parent. We all know that we need food, shelter, warmth, sufficient sleep and so on, if we are to survive and thrive, but our emotional needs are extremely important too. Research has shown that when these needs aren't met, we get over-stressed, can't cope and may even become mentally or physically ill.

Our most important emotional needs have been identified as:*

- security – a sense of being safe and free from undue fear;

- control – a sense of having some degree of control over our lives;

- attention – giving and receiving due attention;

- intimacy – having an emotional connection with at least a few people with whom we can experience friendship, love or fun;

- connection to a wider community – belonging to something bigger than ourselves;

- achievement and status – a feeling that we are competent in important areas of our lives, and that this is recognised within the various groupings to which we belong, such as family, work colleagues or friends;

- privacy – having some time to ourselves;

- relaxation and downtime – time to do things we enjoy while leaving everyday worries aside;

* These needs have been identified by Joe Griffin and Ivan Tyrrell as part of the Human Givens approach to wellbeing (for more details of this approach and books on the subject, see Recommended reading, pages 200–201).

- a sense of meaning and purpose to our lives – through stretching ourselves, giving to others or believing in a power that is greater than ourselves.

We all try to get our needs met in one way or another – one person may get a sense of achievement and status out of becoming a distinguished academic, while another may become a gang leader in order to meet the same need. As parents, we want to help our children meet their needs in positive ways that are in line with our values. We want our children to become useful, caring members of society.

Psychologist Dorothy Rowe talks about one fundamental human need that sums up all the rest. This is the need to preserve and validate our identity – our sense of self. Our greatest fear, according to Rowe, is to feel annihilated as a person. When we feel secure, have some control over what happens to us, give and receive positive attention, feel respected and have a sense of achievement, our sense of self is validated.

Children's needs

Young children let us know straight away when they feel that their needs aren't being met! They cry, scream, have tantrums or sulk. That is all that this behaviour is about. And yes, there is a big difference between what children need and what they want, which we will discuss in the following pages.

Kids learn by using their bodies to try out things themselves (given the chance, they poke their fingers into holes, wriggle through small spaces, etc.) and so they need time for free exploration and play. They also learn by copying us and by asking us questions and trying to make sense of our replies. It is best for kids to have some unstructured time every day, under loose adult supervision, to allow them to develop in their own way and at their own pace. They need a safe environment in which they can play, develop their imagination and learn through trial and error and repetition.

Children's emotional wellbeing is dependent on having a caring adult with whom they can develop a healthy bond in their first few years. Babies are programmed to bond with the adult caring for them, usually their mother. When this caring adult meets their physical and psychological needs, children grow to trust the people around them, and to experience the world as a secure place.

In their early years, children start developing their sense of self. They depend on the people around them to help them make sense of who they are. When children feel loved and respected, they learn to see themselves as worthy of love and respect. When they achieve things they start seeing themselves as little people who 'can do' and develop their self-confidence.

Kids decide early on in their lives whether they are clever or stupid, popular or unpopular, pretty or ugly, weak or strong, musical or tone-deaf, creative or boring, cool or geeky. They also make decisions about the world and about other people: for example, a little girl may decide that her parents love her older sister more than they love her, and therefore believe that she is not good enough. This decision does not necessarily reflect reality, but it seems true to the little girl. Some of the decisions that children make about themselves and about life lie quietly in their sub-conscious minds for years later, running their adult lives, without them even realising it. So, on some level they may still think of themselves as ugly or stupid, even if they have blossomed into beauties or hold down a demanding job, or they may believe that they are not good enough even if this is very far from the truth.

During the first few years of their lives, parents and siblings have by far the strongest influence on how children feel and think. And children are constantly learning, whether it is what you want them to learn or something completely different. Indeed, what they learn about themselves and the world is not always what you think they are learning. Fortunately, when you develop a good understanding of your children's perspective as well as acquire some practical skills, you are well placed to help them develop a healthy sense of self and a positive outlook on life.

Seeing what we think we see

We all react to things in different ways and give meaning to what happens in a manner that is unique to us. And so, we experience our needs as being met or not according to the meaning that we give events, not just according to what happens.

For instance, you will have heard about people who feel financially insecure despite having far more money than most of us would need to feel wonderfully secure. It is not the amount of money that one has that determines whether one feels rich or poor. It is people's belief about how much money they need compared to what they have that is important. Given the same amount of money, some people feel financially secure and some do not. So it is not just the reality of your bank account that determines whether your need for security is being met. It is also your beliefs about this reality, or the meaning that you give it that determines how you feel.

Another example: have you ever sat with a group of friends when one of you made a remark that had some people laughing while others found the same words offensive or distasteful? The same event was interpreted very differently by different people – some heard a joke while others heard an insult. The words were the same but the meaning that different people gave these words varied. The result was that at that particular moment, some people were amused while others became upset. On some level, the people who got upset may have felt that their needs were not being met – perhaps their need to be respected, or the need to belong or to connect to the person who made the joke, or to the rest of the group.

Because people are different, they each see the same reality in their own unique way.

Children are no different in this respect – the same exam grade will be a triumph to one child and a disappointment to another. It is how children understand their exam results that determines whether they perceive that their need to feel successful is being met. I am sure you can come up with plenty of other examples of this sort of thing yourself.

How this affects needs being met

This is hugely important for parents to understand. When children feel that their needs are being met they are generally happy. On the other hand, when they feel that their needs are not being met they can become angry or miserable. Children's happiness is dependent on whether, in their experience, their needs are being met, and this has to do with the meaning that *they* assign to what happens to them. It is not just about the facts.

Take, for example, the need for control: easy-going children may not mind when their dad asks them to tie their shoelaces – they may just shrug and comply, or even enjoy their dad's attention. For these children, at this particular time, tying their shoelaces or not does not have any bearing on their perception of being in control. Another child may perceive the same request as an attempt at control, and therefore refuse and throw a tantrum. The whole family may end up angry and resentful.

Another example: children may feel scared in situations that you know are safe for them, for example, when you leave them for a little while with a family member they do not know very well. Their need to *feel* secure is not met while in reality they are very secure indeed.

Or children may misunderstand our good intentions. We often talk to our children in order to explain things to them, but our words are sometimes interpreted as criticism. When children think they are being criticised by their parents, their need for respect is not being met and they become irritated and resentful. We, as parents, do not see the reasons for this upset as we are focused on our good intentions, not on the meaning that our children put on what we say. Our children perceive a threat to their sense of self yet we see nothing of the sort. They act up and we blame them for being ungrateful.

Bridging the gap

Because the way we experience reality is different from the way our children experience it, it is not enough for us to meet our children's needs in the way that feels right for *us*. We have to meet our children's needs in a way that feels right for *them*.

Often parents believe that they know what their children need based on their own childhood experience. Some parents have predominantly happy childhood memories and would like to make sure that their children's childhood is happy in the same way. Other parents have had difficult experiences during their early years, which they are determined to protect their children from. So parents who enjoyed a particular sport often insist that their children do the same, regardless of the child's inclination, and others who had few material possessions when they were young work long hours to give their children everything money can buy. These parents then feel bitterly disappointed when their children become angry and resentful instead of appreciative and grateful. Little Harry may hate football and want to play chess instead, and little Lucy needs time with her dad, yet instead he is out working so that he can buy her things she does not care much about.

Similarly, many children do not sense our love for them and our investment in them to the degree that we wish they would, simply because we give our love in ways that come naturally to us but don't come across as 'love' to them. We may spend hours expressing our love by doing things for our children, such as making nice meals or tidying away after them. Often, children do not appreciate this – they would rather eat something far simpler and spend more time with us, and they hate what they see as us messing with their belongings.

When the gap between how we see the world and how our children see it is too wide, life can become very difficult for everybody. We get exhausted, feeling that our children's needs are like a bottomless pit – no matter how much we give, nothing seems to be right. At the same time our children feel that their needs are not being met – according to the way they interpret what is happening, they are not getting enough positive attention, respect or love. We feel our children do not appreciate what we do for them and they feel we do not understand.

Our task, as I see it, is to put our own childhood experiences aside and concentrate on what it is that our children need right now. The communication skills explained in the second part of the book will help you achieve this.

Meeting your own needs

We sometimes forget that parents are human and that they need to take care of their own needs too. Many parents, especially mothers, tend to forget about themselves and put their children's needs first. Indeed, it is essential that parents do this for much of the time so that their children are well cared for. However, when parents ignore their own needs for long periods, they become exhausted, and everybody around them, including their children, pays the price.

If you don't look after yourself, you are likely to end up tired, stressed, irritable, frustrated and resentful. You will lose your temper easily and over little things, or feel low and depressed. You will not be a fun person to be around nor a good role model for your children!

Go through the list on pages 15–16, and score how *your* needs are being met at present – with 1 being 'very badly, if at all' and 7 being 'extremely well'. If you score 3 or lower on any one of them, you should think what you can do about it. A lot of low scores from parents are particularly to do with not having enough time to themselves to relax, to spend with other people, to learn new things and such like.

If that's the case for you too, aim to discuss this with your friends and family and think about whether there are any practical steps you can take. Is there anyone who could take care of your children for a while to give you respite? Could you turn to your parents, neighbours or friends? Can you get paid help? You are not being selfish by asking people to help you, and remember that you can always offer help to them in return. Most people genuinely enjoy contributing to other people's lives. Children benefit from this too – they connect to more people and have more fun.

There is also help available online in the form of websites for parents, mostly mums, with lively chat rooms and discussion forums. Parents are there for support and advice, and to show you that you are not on your own in all this. The big advantage to these is that you do not need to get a babysitter and leave home to connect to other parents. (See Websites for parents on pages 202–203.)

If you think you may be unduly anxious, angry, depressed or suffering from addiction you may wish to look at the list of books on pages 200–201, which offer practical advice about managing these issues and better meeting your needs. And of course, you may wish to consult your GP about any concerns you may have.

It is impossible to be a good parent when your own battery is completely flat. You need to allow yours to recharge in whatever way is suitable for you!

Your needs as a couple

If you are raising your children with a partner, you also need to think whether you are investing enough time in your relationship as a couple. You will have much more patience and energy for your children if the two of you can spend enjoyable time together when the kids are not around. Spending time together need not be expensive or complicated. Simple pleasures such as going for a walk in the park or having a drink together can make a lot of difference to your relationship.

You may think, 'Easier said than done,' but, if you have no family around, perhaps you could exchange babysitting services, or arrange sleepovers for your children, with other parents of children of a similar age. Your children will benefit from this too, not just because you will be more relaxed parents but through having more people involved in their lives. They, too, need to have a sense of belonging, not just to their family but also to a wider community.

Your children learn from you what a couple's relationship is about. One of the useful lessons you can teach them is that your relationship with your partner exists outside of your role as parents. You have your friends and your other interests in the same way that they have theirs.

CHAPTER 2

Why do children misbehave?

Co-operation is on the top of most parents' wish list. 'If only my children listened to me! If only they would do what they're told without me having to nag endlessly,' we all say, 'life would be so much easier!' Not only is it easier for parents when their children co-operate, but it is also easier for the children. Believe it or not, children are eager to please and want to be good. So, why don't they just behave themselves? One possible reason is lack of consistency from parents, which we will discuss in the following chapter. Apart from this, there are three main reasons worth considering. See if you can relate any of these points to your own family situation.

An inappropriate way to meet genuine needs

Our children's behaviour, no matter how outrageous, is always an attempt to get genuine needs met. This doesn't mean that all behaviour is okay! Very often it isn't. But the need *behind* the behaviour is genuine, even when it seems designed to annoy.

No child wakes up in the morning and thinks, 'It's a beautiful day! The sun is shining. The birds are singing. I'm looking forward to going to school. Now, time to get on my parents' nerves!' If your children are being annoying, it is because something is not going well for them. Remember, it is all about how your child perceives what is happening rather than just about the facts.

Here are some examples of genuine needs behind inappropriate behaviour:

"I'm starving!"

"I need to stand up for myself!"

Usually, when we are faced with our children's inappropriate behaviour, or what we see as unreasonable requests, our first reaction is not to think about their needs. Instead we get annoyed with them and tell them off or threaten or shout. Or we endlessly explain to them what they already know. When children misbehave, their problem is rarely lack of information, so our explanations generally fall on deaf ears.

These types of response, albeit natural or well intentioned, are the enemy of effective problem solving. If we feel lectured to, criticised or blamed, we usually try to defend and justify ourselves – and children are no different in this respect from adults. Sometimes, they feel so attacked that they even attack back. Looking at children's inappropriate behaviour as a misguided attempt to get genuine needs met can take the heat out of the situation and make it easier to help them learn to meet their needs in ways that *are* appropriate.

A clash of agendas

It is in children's natures to do what they want when they want it, while our job is to help them do the right thing. Parents and children have different agendas, which often clash. (For more on this subject, see *When Your Kids Push Your Buttons* by Bonnie Harris – Recommended reading, page 200.)

Children are not born to eat with a knife and fork, to say please and thank you or to love doing their homework. Their nature is to get what they want whenever they want it, which usually involves a lot of mess and unlimited access to us, on their own terms. But children have to be able to fit into society, so they need to learn when and where various behaviours are appropriate. Why is it okay to lick your ice-cream but not your sandwich? What is wrong with walking naked in the street? And why on earth do people need to make their beds in the morning, only to unmake them to sleep in them at night? We somehow expect our children to happily accept that this is how things are and just get on with it. But it is not in children's nature to do these things, no matter how good our reasons.

Spirited children usually have a greater need for control over what happens to them than easy-going children, which means that it is much more important to them to get their own way. A part of our job as parents is to teach our children to do the right thing, according to our culture and values. Unsurprisingly, the two agendas often clash, and the scene is set for disobedience and misbehaviour.

A way to get attention

The third main reason for children's lack of co-operation is to do with how we manage them. Consider this typical family scenario: When everything is going well, we tend to ignore our children. This is completely understandable, given the million and one things we need to get through each day.

When things go wrong, we spring into action...

Reacting to a crisis is natural – it is our way of keeping our children safe and teaching them how to behave – and I am not for one minute suggesting that you ignore a child in distress. However, the result of reacting too quickly too often to the mundane, frustrating events of everyday life is that we unwittingly teach children that shouting or crying will get them immediate attention. Getting attention is a basic human need and children will do whatever is easiest to see that this need is met. Our reactions teach them to shout or cry – however minor the problem.

To put it simply, you get more of what you pay attention to. If you pay a lot of attention to negative behaviour, you are reinforcing it. If you overreact to minor things that go wrong, you are disempowering your children, unintentionally teaching them that they cannot cope without you. It therefore must make better sense to *reduce* the attention you give to misbehaviour and have a more low-key response when children get frustrated. At the same time, you need to increase the attention you give to *positive* behaviour in order to reinforce that instead.

Unfortunately, ignoring misbehaviour isn't the answer because doing the wrong thing can be great fun for kids and be rewarding in itself. Bad behaviour rarely goes away just by depriving it of attention. Wise parents will do their best to anticipate setbacks and prevent them from happening in the first place. They will also develop a thoughtful, measured response to misbehaviour, and help their children to learn from their mistakes. You will see how this can be done in the following chapters.

CHAPTER 3

The family management team

Does the scenario below look familiar to you? It happens in so many homes. The little boy feels like having a snack but his mum has a different agenda.

The little boy is not giving up. Not having got what he wanted from his mum, he is going to try his dad (see opposite). Parents may not like it, but this is a very natural thing for a child to do.

Why did Dad give in? Perhaps he was preoccupied, perhaps he wasn't aware that dinner was coming, and perhaps he couldn't resist his son's pester power. It is hardly surprising that Mum got upset and the two parents ended up arguing.

The boy did not mean to get his parents to fight with each other. He just tried to get what he wanted when he wanted it. It is not his fault that each of his parents had a different way of responding to his request.

Pushing parents apart

When parents argue in this way, it is usually because they are operating according to their own personality and beliefs rather than in tandem. In many homes, for instance, one parent routinely takes the role of the positive, fun 'softie' while the other takes the role of the firm disciplinarian. The softer the softie is, the more the disciplinarian feels he or she has to discipline, 'otherwise the children will have no respect and no manners'. Yet the more the disciplinarian parent tries to keep structures and boundaries, the more the softie rebels: 'They are just kids. Let them enjoy themselves! Where is the fun in this house? It's just rules and more rules!'

When reading about families or attending parenting classes, parents tend to pick up on the skills that go more naturally with the role that they already have in the family. The softie *loves* being positive and finds it easy to understand the children's needs and feelings, while the disciplinarian feels more comfortable clinging to rules, rewards and consequences. Each becomes locked into the roles that they have made for themselves, and the parents become more and more polarised and more and more resentful of each other. So it is the skills that are *less* natural to us that are actually the ones that we most need to learn.

When a child's behaviour triggers an argument between their parents or other adults that care for them, everybody loses out. The adults get angry and blame each other. They often perceive their child as manipulative, and resent him or her for 'making them fight'. The child is frightened to see adults shouting or arguing and is scared of this new found power. Sisters and brothers resent whichever child is causing the problem, as well as being unsettled themselves. In short: a big mess!

A
MESS

Conflict between parents

We all know that conflict between parents is bad for kids but not everybody understands why and to what extent.

Your child instinctively knows that he or she is 'made' of both of you – you could say 50 per cent from each one of you. When one of you criticises the other, on some level the child feels as if one half of him or herself is criticising the other half. The child's sense of self is challenged as a result of the internal struggle between different parts of the *self*.

On top of that, your child may ask him or herself difficult questions: 'Can Mum love me even though I am half Dad, and she just said that Dad is useless? And in the same way, can Dad love me if he thinks Mum is hysterical, and I am half made of Mum? I love Dad and I love Mum, but Mum doesn't like Dad. So how can I love Dad if she doesn't?' If you are confused by all this, be sure that your child is too.

You may be thinking – 'Hey, hold on a minute, we just have little arguments! Who said we don't love each other? Isn't this taking things a bit too far?' *You* probably know that letting off a bit of steam does not mean that your relationship with your partner is doomed. But your children live in the moment. They don't have the perspective that you do on your relationship with their other parent. They may understand intellectually that parents sometimes fight and then make up and all is well again, but shouting and strong emotions will have much more impact on them than this intellectual knowledge. On some level, your children will react to what they see and hear, not to the explanation you give them.

It is not rare for children of arguing parents to fear that their parents will divorce. They then start worrying about not seeing one parent or missing the other or become terrified of other aspects of an imaginary split. Young children take everything personally, and blame themselves for anything bad that happens, and so they will typically blame themselves for their parents' arguments. This can feel very scary indeed. Their basic need for security is threatened, which may affect other areas of their lives. Children may get into trouble at school or become anxious and clingy, not always able to articulate why. And parents may not connect this to a previous nasty exchange between them – after all, they have already made up and forgotten about the whole incident.

When parents often fight or criticise each other in front of their children, the certain casualties are the children themselves.

None of us is perfect, and we may sometimes end up arguing or criticising each other in front of our kids no matter how much we try to avoid it. If this happens, we can minimise the damage by making sure that our children see us making up. We can have a family hug to reassure them that all is okay now.

Working as a team

Not surprisingly, when adults' relationships are loving and respectful, and they agree among themselves about how to raise their children, both in principle and in practice, children feel more secure and are generally happier. This is true not just for parents but also for stepparents, grandparents, other extended family members, family friends and teachers.

The adults in the illustration below are the family management team, working together to manage their children and their family life. They do not have more value or more importance than their children, but they have a different role – they are in charge. (If you are a single parent, there may be just one of you at the top here or, alongside you, someone who plays a strong part in helping parent your children, such as, perhaps, your mother or sister or brother.)

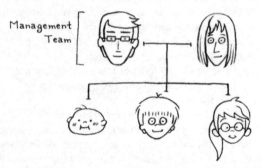

If you are to be a good management team, you need to be united in your efforts. And, unsurprisingly, that means finding compromises. As with any compromise, it will be different from what each one of you ideally wishes for but is a middle way that is sufficiently acceptable to both of you.

Parents who are dealing with challenging child behaviour need to find time regularly, when the children are not around, to sit together and discuss what they want to do. Why not sit somewhere cosy together after the children are finally in bed, get comfortable with a glass of wine or cup of tea and have a chat?

The following four-point discussion plan can help you make the most of your conversations:

1 Start by acknowledging any improvement in the way you managed your kids or in their behaviour. If you look for something positive, you will find it! Give this a few minutes.

2 Describe the problem you want to tackle, to make sure you both know what it is. Stick to one problem every day. Give this one or two minutes only.

3 Think about your children's point of view – what needs are they trying to meet by their behaviour? How may your requests and your communication be perceived? Give this a few more minutes.

4 Discuss your ideas for improving the situation. The second part of the book will give you plenty of tried and tested skills to use. You can use the table on pages 130–32 as a guide through this process. Write down your plans so that you will remember what you decided to do. Give this up to ten minutes.

I know that this is not easy to do in a permanent state of exhaustion, but if you keep these conversations short and concentrate on needs and solutions rather than on problems, you will find that this is time well spent. Getting the two parents aligned is the way to keep relationships healthy and the family functioning well.

Parents who are not together

You may be separated from your children's other parent as a result of divorce or bereavement, or maybe you have never lived together. But if the other parent is around and involved in your children's lives you need to establish yourself as a parenting management team. This is easier to achieve if the separation was amicable and you are on good terms with each other. It is far harder, of course, if your relationship with your ex-partner is still painful.

When separation wounds are raw and emotions are high, it is extremely difficult to put these aside and put the children's needs first. However, this is a necessity for your children. They love and need you both and any conflict between you and your ex-partner creates a conflict inside them. In addition to coping with the practicalities of living in two separate households, children whose parents are separated must come to terms with the fact that their parents do not love each other anymore, and that, most probably, they do not have free access to both parents in the way they used to. This is not easy for a child.

Children can and do recover from their parents splitting up and it is far easier for them to do so when parents manage the split in a way that minimises their children's exposure to conflict. If you do not have a friendly relationship with your ex-partner, you need to establish a business-like relationship instead. Indeed, you are both in the business of raising your children to the best of your ability.

You and your ex-partner are likely to have different opinions about what your children's needs are. This is to be expected. Also, you are unlikely to achieve the level of consistency that is possible in households where the two parents live together, so your child will have to learn that different houses have different rules.

It is important to remember, however, that more than any detail about their routine or about what they do in each household, children need parents who communicate with each other respectfully, and who do not bad-mouth each other. If you feel unable to talk together without the conversation deteriorating into a row, use email or text each other and stick to children's issues while putting aside everything else. Don't ask your children to pass messages on to your ex – this puts far too much pressure on them.

Unfortunately, you cannot make sure that your ex-partner will take part in your business-like parenting team, but you can take some steps that will make this more likely to happen. The next section is relevant for parents who are in disagreement, whether they are together or apart, and will give you some ideas to consider. If you feel that you are unable to communicate with your ex-partner civilly, I encourage you to seek professional help.

Being a single parent brings extra challenges of its own, which are outside of the scope of this book. See Recommended reading, page 201, for further reading.

Parents who won't work in the team

If the other parent is not willing to work with you as a team, the first question to ask yourself is why this is happening. Why does your partner, or ex-partner, not want to participate in your management team with you? After all, he or she also loves the children and knows that it is important that you are both united.

My experience of working with parents shows that there are

two common reasons for a parent being unwilling to work in the team. By far the most typical is that one parent feels criticised by the other. And it is usually the women who complain about the men and criticise the way they do things. The men are told off for little misdemeanours: getting children into the wrong outfit, forgetting to make sure that they brush their hair, giving them pasta for lunch instead of heating up carefully prepared organic quinoa or opening a carton of orange juice when there is one already open. Women want men to do things exactly the way that they do them, and men can't, or they won't.

Remember that you each see the same reality in different ways. When a woman tells a man that she wants to talk, the man often hears that she wants to complain. And, not surprisingly, he feels like running away. And when women explain to men why they should do things their way, men usually feel that they are being controlled or not trusted, and so instinctively wish to do just the opposite. Many men despair of ever being able to please women, no matter how hard they try.

The second common reason for parents – whether male or female – not wanting to engage in the management team is that they believe that strategies agreed on previously were not followed through. You may both have agreed about no sweets, or no TV after 7pm, but one of you gave in to your children or just forgot about the agreement. As a result, the other one feels undermined, while the parent who gave in probably feels guilty, incompetent or resentful if the other parent is 'always right'.

The secret to getting the other parent on board is for you to understand that you too need to change your own attitude. If you want your partner to be a part of the team, do your best not to criticise, especially when the kids are in earshot. Think of solutions, not past problems. Ask for your partner's ideas – they are as important as yours. Suggest your ideas rather than insist that things are done your way. Acknowledge your partner's efforts even if you do not completely agree with that way of doing things. Do your utmost to stick to your agreement and readily admit if you slip up.

If you feel that your approach to raising kids is different from your partner's for whatever reason, I encourage you to discuss together the ideas in this book. It will help you clarify your thinking, give you practical strategies for dealing with problems and bring your parenting approaches closer together. And if you have found this section particularly relevant to you, why not be brave and start by discussing it with your partner?

CHAPTER 4

Principles of positive change

Improving your understanding of how families and relationships work will put you in a better position to deal with the changing demands that parenting brings. Consider the principles in this chapter and their relevance to your own family situation and see how taking them on board can make a difference to you and your children.

Taking into account *everybody's* needs

Unfortunately, many of us believe that meeting one person's needs has to come at the expense of those of others. This thinking usually leads to power struggles.

"MY needs...!"

Instead, if you assume that it is always possible to get everyone's needs better met, a whole domain of creative possibilities will open up for you. You will now be able to look at the problem as an opportunity for you all to create something new that will serve everyone.

Behind every want there is a valid need

We all tend to confuse what we want with what we need. To be more precise, we experience our wants as needs. 'I need a new handbag!' I think. But do I? And do I need a new laptop, or yet another pair of shoes, or a bag of lightly salted crisps in the middle of the night?

Children, too, experience their wants as needs. They 'need' to wear this particular pair of jeans but not the other, have the latest game for their latest electronic gadget, or to go to the park now, not in five minutes.

It is easy to dismiss these demands as evidence of children being spoiled, and get into endless arguments with them. However, it may be useful to consider that behind anything that you or your children want, there is a valid need that you wish to fulfil. Otherwise, why would you want it?

Children may feel a need to wear a particular pair of jeans or play a particular game in order to have a sense of belonging with their peer group. They may want to go to the park now and not later because they need to have a sense of control over what is happening or because they cannot wait to get to the park to meet their need for play and exercise.

This does not mean that children, or adults, should always get what they want – not at all. But looking for the needs behind your wants opens up more possibilities for meeting these needs in other ways. The friends may not mind the wrong jeans so much, and it is possible for children to feel they belong to their group of friends even if they don't own a particular electronic game. Maybe they can think of something else they can do with their friends, or perhaps they can occasionally play the game in a friend's house. The child desperate to go to the park now and not later can have the need for control satisfied by having something to do to keep him or her busy while waiting for you to get ready, together with a clear idea of when you are going to leave.

The illusion of control

Many of us wrongly believe that it is possible to discipline children so that they will always do what we ask. In the not-so-good-old days, parents used physical punishments to achieve this, not necessarily successfully. Our generation replaced the rod with reasoning. 'If we only explain what we want well enough,' we think in a mixture of anticipation and desperation, 'our children will understand our position and will do what we ask.' Sometimes our explanations are effective and our children eventually do what we request, but at other times they do not. Children have a different agenda from ours and they may stick to it, no matter how much we reason with them. The more we explain, the more they believe that we are trying to control them and the more they are tempted to rebel.

Life becomes easier when you adjust your expectations and accept that there is no way that you can control the thoughts or actions of other people, not even those of your children. When your children are small you may be able to pick them up and put them in their car seat kicking and screaming, but you cannot make them eat, sleep, stop crying or smile. Similarly, you cannot make older children do what you ask without their being willing to do it first. Thinking that you can make your children do what you want against their will is an illusion. I shall call it the illusion of control.

So your children, in much the same way as adults, must be *willing* to do what you ask them to do if they are to do it. They need to be motivated to act. And the best way to motivate children is to connect whatever it is that you want them to do with their *own* needs. Children are not particularly interested in your needs. They are far more interested in their own.

Does letting go of the illusion of control mean that you cannot influence your children? Not at all. In fact, influencing children is exactly what this book is about. You can influence children by helping them see that their needs are better met when they co-operate with you. Fortunately, one of your children's strongest needs is for approval from you – they want to be good in your eyes. When you show children that you appreciate their effort to do the right thing, they will be motivated to do it more. Over time, they will behave better and better.

A long-term view

The process of getting children to co-operate with you is long and often not easy. Children need to learn to behave in ways that are unnatural for them, at least initially. It is not natural for children to hang their coat on the peg or to wait until you finish talking with your friend in order to talk to you, or to stop what they are doing and come with you because you are in a hurry. They need to *learn* to do all that, and learning something new always takes time.

Your challenge as parents is to achieve co-operation while keeping warm relationships with your children and supporting their sense of self-worth. Parents of spirited children usually find this more difficult as their children are more impulsive and do not easily learn from their experience. There is no magic wand. It takes as long as it takes.

If you accept that progress may be slower than you wish, you will be able to keep your calm. As long as you are progressing, even by tiny little steps, you are doing fine. There is no need to forget your standards and expectations – they can be very useful as long-term goals.

Avoiding arguments

There is no way a parent can win an argument with a child. When an argument finishes, there will always be *two* losers. Even if the parent had a good point that the child eventually conceded – which very few children ever do – the child is probably feeling hurt and humiliated. When children lose arguments they doubt themselves and their ability, question their parent's love for them, and often secretly plot their revenge. Is this the victory that you want? I'm sure it is not. By 'winning' arguments with your children (or with any other person) you threaten their sense of self-worth and your relationships with them. You may win the particular argument but you lose the relationship.

Children cannot win arguments either – when parents give in to them under pressure, children may feel a temporary sense of achievement. But at the same time, on another level, they experience too much power and that is scary and unhealthy for them. On top of this, they now have to deal with a frustrated parent, who may be resentful and unaffectionate towards them for a while. In the long term this is not a victory either. Wise parents avoid arguments at all costs.

People have a strong drive to be right and to win. No one wants to be shown to be wrong. Our sense of achievement and status are likely to be hurt when we lose. Children equate losing an argument with being wrong, weak, bad, incompetent, a failure or all of these. Parents are often guilty of that too.

We sometimes act as if we live on an imaginary narrow ladder, with the winner at the top and the loser at the bottom. We struggle to position ourselves at the top by being right and making sure the other person knows that they are wrong.

The ladder is a very sad place to live. No one can ever relax there, as all their time and energy goes into power struggles and competition. If we want to be happy, we'd better throw the ladder away by giving up the idea that one person must be right and the other one wrong. Instead of arguing and trying to win, we need to think of ways to resolve the issue at hand so that everybody feels respected and valued.

Often we don't mean to argue – we seem to drift into arguments without realising that it is happening. Arguments frequently start when we notice a child's mistake or see that a child is struggling with something. With the best of intentions, we make a comment, but this is when things start to go wrong.

Pointing out mistakes

Many parents think that when they notice a problem in their children's behaviour, they need to point it out to them, so that their children can put it right. However, children often interpret this differently – they hear criticism. Children need to feel that they are competent, and this perceived criticism makes them feel that they have failed. They then defend themselves either by ignoring their parent or by answering back. Yet another drama begins. Have a look at the following example.

Some children may not react so strongly. They may simply correct their mistake and move on. However, they may well be thinking, 'I got it wrong again' or 'I'm rubbish at spelling' or 'No matter how much I try, it's never good enough'. Spirited children who have been criticised a lot in the past are even more sensitive and may react to the tiniest hint of disapproval in their parent's body language or tone of voice.

Many parents are now mindful not to criticise their children's character. Instead, they criticise their children's actions, just like the parent in the picture above, who corrected his son's spelling mistake. Telling his son that he made a mistake is indeed far better than telling him that he is lazy, stupid or bad. Unfortunately, however, his son may interpret the correction to mean all of these things anyway.

How do you feel when your boss, your sibling or your mother-in-law shows you where you went wrong? Do you feel grateful for the information and want to hear more, so that you can improve yourself? I doubt it. We all find it hard to hear about our shortcomings. Imagine how children, being vulnerable and immature, must feel when we point out their mistakes.

Criticism comes at a price to children's self-esteem and to their relationship with their parents. If you wish your children to be more confident in their abilities, you need to correct them in a way that will enhance their self-esteem. And, if you want your children to want to be around you and listen to what you have to say, you need to speak in ways that are pleasant for them to hear.

You may be wondering how this can be done and how your children will improve if you do not point out their mistakes. Descriptive praise (see Chapter 5) will enable you to correct your children's mistakes in a constructive way that does not damage their self-esteem. (The example on pages 56–57 shows how this can be done.)

Don't give up

When the same problems occur over and over, we understandably feel overwhelmed, frustrated, confused, exasperated and fed up! We sometimes wish we could just ignore the whole thing and make it go away. However, problems rarely disappear of their own accord. To make problems go away, we need to think of new ways of dealing with them, taking into account everyone's needs.

You get more of what you pay attention to, so if you focus on problems, you will see more and more problems. But if you believe that there is always a way to make thing better, you will see a route forward. Keep this idea in mind, almost like a mantra, and you will continue to find new ideas and ways to improve situations, no matter how hopeless things may seem at first. Explain this new mantra to your children too. Show them that even when things are tough, you don't give up!

Your job as parents

Over time, your job as parents changes. When your children are very young, the task is to meet all their physical and psychological needs. As your children grow and develop, your job develops too – to help them build their own resources so that they can gradually meet more and more of their needs themselves.

There is an ongoing dilemma built into this job – on the one hand you want your children to know that you love and accept them unconditionally, no matter what they do. Yet on the other hand you must teach them to behave in ways that fit with your culture and values.

This is the fine line that all parents need to tread.

PART 2

Positive skills to improve children's behaviour and self-esteem

Having looked into human needs and family dynamics in the first part of this book, you are now ready to learn some new positive communication skills. These will help you develop and keep good relationships with your children while motivating them to behave well. The skills work because they help you get your point across as parents while being mindful of your children's perspective and needs.

This part of the book will give you skills to:

- improve children's behaviour and self-esteem;

- minimise resistance when your agendas clash;

- handle strong emotions – yours and your children's;

- prepare for success, so that it is more likely to happen;

- get your children to want to do the right thing;

- learn from mistakes;

- take the heat out of sibling rivalry;

- better enjoy your leisure time.

CHAPTER 5

Descriptive praise

The first positive communication skill to learn is one known as descriptive praise. It is an incredibly useful and simple-to-learn skill yet most parents do not know about it. Instead, they tend to give praise in a way that, unfortunately, is not very helpful.

I will start by explaining why the most common type of praise parents give their children is not particularly effective. You will then see how to use descriptive praise when your child is already doing something that you like, and how you can use the same skill to correct mistakes.

How not to praise your child

Adults often praise children by saying 'Good boy!', 'This is fantastic!' or 'Clever girl!'. Any praise is better than criticism, of course, but it has been shown that this kind of praise (called evaluative praise because it makes a judgement about children or their actions) is not very effective in building children's self-esteem, and does not usually motivate them to behave well.

There are several reasons for this:

- When you look at your daughter's drawing and say enthusiastically, 'This is wonderful, you are so talented!', you are in fact giving her your own opinion as if it were the truth. Children have opinions of their own and they do not necessarily agree with our point of view. Your daughter may know that her work cannot be that wonderful as she often sees that other children around her have done even better. She probably thinks that you say this because you are her parent and you love her, not because she really deserves it. It is good for her to feel your love and approval. But at the same time you miss an opportunity to say something about her drawing that she would believe, and that would build her self-esteem.

- When you say 'Good boy' or 'You are so great', children do not always know what they are being praised for, as this kind of praise contains very little information about what they did right. It is important that they know what is being praised, so that they can repeat the good behaviour again and again.

- When you say to children that they are clever, talented or smart they may think that their intelligence rather than their effort is the reason for their achievement, so they can see no reason to put any effort into what they do. We all know bright children who won't tackle anything unless it seems easy to them; it is as if they think that they can only be clever if they can complete a task with no effort at all. Trying to tackle a difficult task also carries the risk of failure, which, in their eyes, may expose them as not so clever any more, so they give up.

What is descriptive praise?

Descriptive praise is very different from evaluative praise. It requires you to describe exactly what it is that you like about your children's behaviour or achievement. To make the best use of it, you need actively to look for things that your children are doing right, even if they are not perfect, and then describe what you see. If you stick to the facts, your children will find it hard to contradict you or argue with you, even in their thinking. You can also give your opinion but should not pretend that it is the truth. Descriptive praise provides information that anyone can see is true ('You have been carrying your bag all the way home by yourself!'), or expresses what you think or feel ('I really like the monster you made out of a tomato'). Who can argue with that?

Almost all children respond to this positive attention by wanting to do more of whatever you descriptively praise. They feel grown-up, accepted and respected, so their self-esteem grows as well. Very occasionally, children act as if they do not like your praise – pages 53–55 will give you some ideas as to what to do when this happens.

On the opposite page in the top illustration this little boy probably feels valued and respected. The little boy in the bottom illustration will feel good about himself and about his mum. He will be more likely to put his plate in the dishwasher in future, especially if his mum remembers to mention this to other friends and relatives when her son is in earshot. He is likely to try to hold his knife and fork properly for a while longer so that he can gain a bit more attention and approval. Mum can reinforce this further by mentioning the knife and fork again, using different words, later on.

Your own children may not be so angelic and may need to be reminded about the dishes. You can still motivate them to improve by using descriptive praise, 'I only had to remind you a couple of times and you are now putting your plate in the dishwasher carefully. Maybe tomorrow you will remember this yourself. What do you think?' Be very careful not to sound sarcastic when you say something like this. It can take a long while for children to learn new habits – it is only to be expected that they will need to be reminded.

Praise small improvements

Do not wait until your child does something wonderful to use descriptive praise. Praising only big achievements is not enough, as they do not happen very often, even for successful kids. To motivate children to do their best and make them feel successful and happy within themselves, you need to praise descriptively even small improvements in their behaviour. Mention any progress, even if your child is not yet achieving the standard that you aim for, while keeping your standards as a long-term goal.

It is the children who are the least successful and confident, because they rarely do things exceptionally well or 'come top' or win things, who are most in need of descriptive praise. These are the children who get less approval from their teachers or peers, so they need to see that you appreciate their efforts and believe they can improve. Even children who are generally successful may have areas in their lives where they are not doing well. This is where they need descriptive praise most, because this is where they will need to put in the most effort.

When children do not seem to achieve much in a particular area, it is probably because things are still difficult for them. If you praise their effort, not just their achievement, they are more likely to make even more effort. This is particularly important for children with physical or learning difficulties, who need to put a lot of time and effort into acquiring skills that come easily to their peers. If you praise them for trying and not giving up, they are more likely to try even more and to take more risks and stretch themselves. Catch your children doing what you want them to do, and then make a big deal out of it.

Remember, you are not telling your children that they have done something wonderful when they haven't. You are simply noticing and complimenting their efforts.

It may not always feel easy to give this sort of praise, either because it seems that your children are not doing enough to 'deserve' it or because you are simply frustrated with their behaviour or lack of achievement. If you find yourself criticising your children or losing your patience, and finding nothing to praise, you are probably inside the negative cycle depicted on page 12. As adults, it is your job to break that cycle.

Examples of descriptive praise

Here are some more ideas of the type of things you can say to your children. You will, or course, need to adapt them to suit your personal style and your children's needs.

Praising improvements

- 'The way you wrote this "h" is very clear. The line is tall enough so I can see that it is not an "n".'

- 'You are opening one eye ... and moving a bit. You are probably realising that it is time to get up ...'

- 'You've remembered one of the things that you need to take with you to school today. I think you're getting better at organising your belongings.'

- 'I love that you started practising the piano without any reminders.'

- 'You remembered to write the date at the top of the page.'

Praising effort

- 'It is not easy for you to open this door, but you keep pushing. You are not giving up easily.'

- 'You really didn't want to answer this maths question but you gave it a go anyway.'

- 'It can be difficult to share your toys with other children, and you are getting better and better at it.'

- 'You are trying this nectarine even though you have never had one before. I can see you are getting more grown up at trying new foods.'

'After attending the parenting session on descriptive praise, I was astonished and amused at some of the examples. Some of them sounded a bit contrived and I just couldn't see myself using them (especially the one that went, "Oh, you've managed to open one eye ..."). "Oh dear," I thought, "even the cat could see through *that* one!"

'The next morning, though, I needed help. After calling and calling, I still couldn't get Charles to come down for his breakfast. When I finally went up to his room, he was still in bed and I couldn't even see his head above the covers.

'I desperately tried to think of examples of descriptive praise for getting out of bed. However, all I could remember was the "one eye". I peeked under the cover and saw one eye glaring at me balefully, so I piped up as cheerfully as I could, "Oh well done! Bravo! You've managed to open one eye!" The glaring eye hesitated; the head lifted and there were two puzzled eyes. "Amazing," I beamed. "I can see *two* eyes. My goodness, two eyes, and so close to each other!" A large chuckle came from the head as it emerged from under the duvet. "Mamma, of course there are two eyes. They're right next to each other!" He continued to giggle as he considered what a face would look like if this weren't the case. He threw back the duvet and descended the ladder from his bunk, chortling merrily.

'In the following weeks, I have used variations of "one eye" every morning. I began to say in a breathless expectant voice, "And will there be a *third* eye?" *That* one induced the giggles to begin *before* the head emerged from the duvet! I drew and cut out a paper eye and stuck it to various bits of him. I then claimed to find it by poking the lumps under the duvet. That got him out of his bed the fastest; he's a very ticklish boy and he loves the ridiculous!'

Teresa, mother of six-year-old Charles

How often to use descriptive praise

Praise young children at least ten times every day. This may seem a lot but if you stick to the facts, describing just what your child is doing and saying how much you like it, your children will not become spoiled. They will feel better in themselves and be motivated to do the right thing more often. Keep praising them into their teenage years, but of course, not nearly as often!

Many families establish time for praise as a part of their bedtime routine. Imagine your children going to sleep with a cuddle and some warm, loving words about their behaviour during the day, delivered in a way that they can actually believe. This surely is one of the best ways to say goodnight.

Getting it right

It is very important to put some effort into making sure that your praise is truly descriptive – that you stick to the facts and, when you give your opinions, you clearly present them as your opinions, not the truth. Since very few of us were brought up on descriptive praise, you may believe that you are using descriptive praise when in fact you are not.

There is another mistake that is easy to make – praising things that are *too* trivial. Children usually let you know if you are doing this.

To use descriptive praise with children who seem resistant, you need to choose your words more carefully.

Some parents say that using descriptive praise feels unnatural at first. They are right! It is *not* our nature to describe what goes well; our nature is to notice what is wrong. But if you start to use descriptive praise even when it feels strange, you quickly get used to it and it will feel more and more natural – just as anything you practise regularly becomes more natural.

Rejection of descriptive praise

While most children love the new descriptive praise, others may initially be suspicious. They ask, 'Why are you talking to me like this?' It can be tempting to stop. Instead, it is better to explain: 'I've realised that I didn't use to notice all the good things that you do, and now I'm trying to change this. I can now see so many things I like and I've decided to tell you what they are.'

Have you ever rejected a compliment, and then secretly enjoyed it later? I remember doing this myself. 'I really like your earrings!' a friend would say. And my response? 'I got them for a few quid at the market stall.' Not very grateful, I admit. The next day, when choosing what earrings to wear I would somehow to be drawn towards the same ones again. 'Maybe they are quite nice after all,' I would think. So, we sometimes find it hard to appreciate a compliment when it is given, but enjoy it later. Your children may be reacting to your descriptive praise in a similar way.

Correcting mistakes

You have seen how descriptive praise can be used to reinforce behaviour that you like, but it can also be used to correct your children's mistakes. The cartoon on page 41 showed how one dad pointed out his son's spelling mistake, and how his son responded by becoming defensive. Here's a different way to deal with the situation.

Dad mentions what his son did right, not what he did wrong. His son feels validated and successful, and is more willing to look at what isn't so perfect.

Dad is careful to minimise the mistake and not make a big deal out of it. He is not giving his son the correct spelling, but is making him think and come up with the answer by himself. In this way, his son learns much better and can be proud when he gets the answer right.

As explained earlier, our natural reaction to new things is usually to notice what is wrong about them. This is what happens when we see a child's piece of work – we can't help noticing the mistakes and the imperfections. Dad in the cartoon suppressed his natural tendency to mention what was wrong and deliberately turned his attention to what was right. He then complimented his son. To use a cliché, Dad was looking at the half of the glass which was full, not the half which was empty. And when he had a good look at the glass, he noticed that it was much fuller than he had realised before! In fact, it was 99 per cent full.

When you point out what your children are doing right, you are meeting their needs for being accepted and for feeling successful. They are then more likely to be open to considering what they got wrong. You can give them a hint as to what to look for (a missing letter) and praise them descriptively again when they work out the answer. This is more rewarding than just telling them the correct spelling. Children learn by trying to solve problems. Giving children the answer ('There is another "r" in "carrot".') may feel helpful, but in fact it takes away their opportunity to figure out the answer for themselves and to feel proud about it.

Getting your children to praise themselves

You are not going to be there, dishing out your descriptive praise forever. Your children need to learn to become confident and proud of themselves, even when you are not around, so they need to learn to notice for themselves improvements in their efforts and achievements. One of the best ways to foster this skill is to ask them simple questions such as, 'What do you like about your work?', 'What are you most proud of?', 'Is there anything else that you think is good about your work that I forgot to mention?' or, if you are doing this at bedtime, 'Is there anything else that you have done well during the day that I did not notice?'

In order to answer these kinds of questions, your children will have to reflect on what they did. Once they start looking carefully at their work, they will start noticing all the things that are good about it, which they may have not noticed before. They are also likely to spot their mistakes without your prompting, and may quickly correct them.

Your children may initially not be very forthcoming. They may say that they don't know what is good about their work, or declare that there is nothing that they like about it. There could be several reasons for this kind of response: your children may not be used to reflecting on their work and may not know what to say. They may be comparing it to others who can do better. Or they may be struggling with issues of self-esteem, and you will need to build it up gradually and not give up! Say, for example: 'This "C" is really round and beautiful. I think it is the best one on the page. What do you think?'

As long as you both stick to the facts and describe what you see, no amount of descriptive praise will make your children 'big-headed'. Instead, it will help them to reflect on what they do and reinforce the positive aspects of their behaviour. The ability to reflect on and appreciate our own achievements is one of the important building blocks for self-esteem.

More reasons to praise

Many parents who start using descriptive praise report that because they are on the lookout for things to praise, they suddenly notice many more things that their children *are* doing right, which makes them appreciate their children even more!

Other parents notice that their children start to use descriptive praise on them. Wouldn't you like your child to thank you for a lovely day out, or thank his little brother for helping out? When you start mentioning things that your children are doing right, they will start doing it too.

'You are colouring inside the lines, just the way the teacher asked. I like that you are taking your time to do it properly.'

'I like your drawing too, Mum. It is beautiful.'

Lisa and her five-year-old son

CHAPTER 6

When your agendas clash

In every family there are times when you want to do one thing and your child wants to do another – your agendas clash. The secret here is to be diplomatic in order to avoid arguments and confrontations while still standing your ground.

Most of us do not think that we are being argumentative or confrontational when we talk with our kids. We try our best not to shout or criticise too much, and to explain things rather than demand obedience. Unfortunately, this is not always enough and we often end up arguing anyway. Remember, there is no way to win an argument with a child – there will always be two losers.

This chapter looks at how communication skills can be used to reduce conflict and prevent upsets from happening in the first place. You will see how to refuse your children's requests in a way that will make it easier for them to accept the refusal, and how to ask for what you want so that your children are more likely to co-operate. Be realistic – your children are unlikely to be happy or gracious about not getting their own way. It is enough that they comply. They are children, and their nature is to get what they want when they want it!

A yes that also means no

For many children, especially the spirited ones, the word 'no' often triggers a huge drama. Children, as well as adults, have a need to feel some degree of control over what happens to them and a 'no' from a parent at once removes all control, which may tempt children to rebel. The trick is to get the message across without saying the word 'no'. When you do this, you all win – your children preserve their sense of control and you get them to do the right thing without too much fuss.

Here is an example of how this can be done. First, the challenging situation – Mum needs to make a request that is unlikely to be popular with her son.

Understandably, Mum is in a hurry; she needs to leave. She may even have left this until the last minute out of consideration towards her son. Unfortunately, her son has another agenda – he wants to play. No child likes leaving what they enjoy doing in order to do something less tempting. Mum's response to her son is understandable but invites conflict.

A simple change to the way she talks to her child can make all the difference.

Mum said yes to her child's request, and then offered a time when he could do what he wanted. You will be surprised how effective this simple strategy is. When you say 'yes' and offer an alternative, children feel that their wishes are respected and are far more willing to co-operate with you. Of course, this communication skill is not guaranteed to work every time, but more often than not it does!

Asking a question

Here's another common scenario that we could tackle differently. The daughter makes a request that Mum is going to refuse. First, here's the natural, yet less helpful, way to communicate this.

Instead of saying no, even with an explanation, Mum can choose to ask a question that will encourage her daughter to think about the situation herself.

Now the girl has to think, and reach the conclusions herself. She is not going to be happy about the situation but she may just accept it.

This way of putting things makes it easier for the little girl to accept that she cannot watch TV. It also provides an opportunity for more descriptive praise from Mum once she has got the answer right!

It is possible that the little girl will not accept the 'no TV' rule. This is covered on pages 93–96, when we look at what strong feelings do to us.

Refusing graciously

Often children make reasonable requests that you have to decline because of your own circumstances. You may even wish you could say yes, but cannot. Who said life is always easy?

Faced with a sudden request like this, which circumstances prevent Dad from accepting, his natural response is to get irritated and tell his daughter off.

Dad's response is completely understandable. How can his daughter expect him to drop everything and do what she asks with virtually no notice? Dad may have loved to hear his daughter play her instrument and is now feeling that he is missing out. It is likely that variations of this scenario have happened at home before, and this is yet another reminder of his daughter's lack of organisational skills and his own lack of control over his schedule. Even though Dad may have good reasons for his response, his words are unlikely to help his relationship with his daughter. Neither are they likely to motivate her to improve her organisational skills.

The girl here regrets having opened her mouth to make the request. Not only is her dad not going to come and listen to her play, she now believes he is angry with her. The chances are that she is not listening to his advice in a way that is helpful. Instead, in her head, she is probably busy defending herself or feeling sorry for herself, while conveniently avoiding looking at her own contribution to the situation. She is a child so she can only see her own point of view.

To prevent unhappy situations like this from developing, follow these guidelines:

- Give your reasons *before* refusing. It is best to explain your circumstances before you refuse the request because the refusal itself is likely to upset your children and they will then be less able to take in any explanations, however reasonable. If you give your reasons first, they are more likely to hear them, and are more likely to accept the situation even when they hate it.

- Explain your needs and do not criticise your children. When explaining why you cannot agree to a request, it is best to talk about what *you* have to do and the circumstances that prevent you from agreeing, rather than laying the blame on what your children have or haven't done. Not getting their own way is a bad enough consequence for kids; they do not need you to rub it in.

- Show your child that you have considered your response and that you understand their side even if you cannot say yes to it.

- Try to avoid saying the word 'no'. Let your children come to understand that they cannot have their way. You can use leading questions to help you with this.

- Make sure you talk about what went wrong at a later time. Learning from mistakes is important. Try to resist the temptation to try to teach your children a lesson when they are too upset to listen. This is discussed in more detail in Chapter 10 Learning from mistakes.

Going back to the example on page 64, this is how Dad can refuse his daughter while minding her feelings and their relationship.

Dad states his needs, does not blame his little daughter, and avoids saying 'no'.

If the little girl continues begging and pleading with Dad, he can repeat how he wishes he could come to her concert, then give her a hug and a kiss, apologise and leave. If Dad has to go, he has to go! Of course, Dad can offer ideas such as getting someone else to record the concert or take his daughter's picture when she performs. The girl may still be upset, but this is unavoidable.

No matter how good Dad's intentions may be, or how frustrated he may feel, this is not the right time to teach better organisation skills or to express his frustration. The girl is too disappointed to listen. He will have plenty of opportunities to discuss how to avoid similar situations at a later time.

Giving limited choice

Your children are more likely to go along with your request if you offer them some choice. What may seem like a token concession to you can make a big difference to your children – it helps them feel that their opinion counts. It is best to offer limited choice, as too much choice can be confusing.

Would you like to leave in 5 or 10 minutes?

You must be careful to offer your children choice only when you are okay with whatever they pick. Sometimes, when we appear to offer choice, we are actually expecting that our children will do what we ask. More often than not, we are disappointed. Questions such as 'Shall we go home?' or 'Would you like to go to bed now?' are not fair unless we are happy to accept a 'no'. We usually speak this way out of politeness but our children feel we are not honest with them. It is better to say instead 'We need to leave in two minutes,' or 'It's time to go to bed'. It is unrealistic to expect children to resist temptation when we offer it. No child wants to choose the healthy, sensible option. Children want the tasty, wacky, fun one! It is your job to remove temptations and make it easy for your children to do what you ask.

Body language and tone of voice

Some children seem to sense the tiniest hint of irritation in our voice or body language, and react to it disproportionately. You will not be surprised to hear that spirited children are usually more sensitive to this than easy-going kids, perhaps because they get criticised a lot and come to expect criticism even when it is not there.

We sometimes think that we need to use an assertive tone of voice when we make a request, to make sure that children know who is boss. Unfortunately, children often react to this by becoming more resentful.

On the other hand, using an artificially calm tone of voice may come across as sarcastic or patronising. I find it more effective to stay below the child's volume of voice. When your children are already shouting, raise your voice a bit but stay below theirs. When they are calmer, be calmer too. You can also get down to your child's eye level or bring your child up to yours. By towering above their children, speaking in a stern voice, you are inviting resentment and rebellion.

Modelling behaviour

None of us likes to be told what to do – we feel we are being 'bossed around' and that our need for control is interfered with. Children do not like it any more than adults. Yet parents I have worked with often say that, on a typical morning, their child gets at least 20 instructions (or the same instruction 20 times). 'Get up. Get dressed. Don't forget to brush your teeth. Put your shoes on. Put your shoes on. Put your shoes on. Hurry up! We are going to be late ...'. I used to be no different – 100 instructions among three children was more like it for me.

Things can go wrong even when we make a simple request.

The girl is probably not cold and feels controlled by her mum. And in her childish way she does what is natural for her to do – she runs off!

To help your kids do the right thing, demonstrate it yourself while describing in words what you are doing. When you model the behaviour you want from your children in this way, they get to see and hear what you are hoping they will do next without being given direct instructions. As a result, any temptation to rebel is reduced. The illustration on the next page shows you how you can do it.

Is it always that easy? Not always. But you will be amazed how often this works, especially with spirited children who seem to be oversensitive to instructions of any kind. The girl is listening to the explanation without any pressure and feels she can choose what to do about it. She is therefore much more likely to do what her mother wants, feeling that she is doing this out of her own choice. Of course, there is no guarantee that she will! You will find many more useful strategies for achieving co-operation in the following chapters.

Making sure your children are listening

Who hasn't shouted instructions at their children from another room and got increasingly frustrated when they did not obey? Because children live in the moment, they find it hard to switch their attention away from whatever they are absorbed in and do what they are asked to do. Unless you get their attention before you speak, they will simply tune you out.

For children to take you seriously, you need to go to where they are. Then they are more likely to look at you and, if they don't, you can get even closer! Then say what you want them to do, using a pleasant tone of voice. They are far more likely to take you seriously if you stay and wait for them to start doing as they are told than if you go away and leave them to it.

'Eye contact is crucial'

'When getting my three girls ready for school, I always felt let down at the last hurdle: they were not putting on their shoes. They always wanted me to find the shoes and do them up.

'Before, I just used to lose it at this point. They had got dressed themselves. They are obviously capable of putting their shoes on too. Why couldn't they just get on with it? I would shout downstairs to them from my bedroom – "Put your shoes on, now!" But they were paying no attention. I would have to do the job myself, resentful and irritated, if we were to get to school on time.

'After the course, I realised that I had to get their attention before asking them to put on their shoes. Would I talk this way to anyone else? To a friend or a work colleague?

'I have now learned that eye contact is crucial when talking to my girls. So, first, I ensured that I got dressed earlier so that I did not need to worry about getting ready myself. I made sure that I got down to the girls' eye level, praised them for having got ready in time and then asked them what they thought the last thing they needed to do was, in order to walk to school. Even if they didn't answer in words, they might look at their shoes, at which point I would say in a big happy voice, "Yes, that's right! You need to put on your shoes. You know exactly what to do." It has made all the difference – the girls just do it and our mornings are much calmer now.'

Fiona, mother of three girls aged four to nine

CHAPTER 7

Emotions and what to do with them

The emotions that cause the upsets in family relationships are, of course, the negative ones. It can be helpful to think of strong emotions such as anxiety, anger and frustration as part of our body's 'alarm system', telling us that something is going wrong and that we need to take action. The trigger for these emotions is usually an expectation that is not being fulfilled – we want to get into our home but cannot find the key, or we expect our children to do what we ask but they ignore us, or we were expecting to have a lovely dinner but we have just burned the rice.

We respond to the 'alarm' by experiencing a sudden sense of urgency as stress hormones are released into the blood stream. Our body prepares to take action to make sure that we keep safe and get what we need.

But when our emotions are high, our intelligence is low. This is especially true when we are angry: our thinking becomes simplistic and we may say and do things that make complete sense to us at the time but appear 'over the top' or downright stupid later. It has to be this way because emotions are part of our ancient survival system. When our ancestors had to flee danger or fight it, there wasn't time to think reasonably or weigh options up – they just had to act!

Children's emotions

Children's brains are less developed than those of adults, so their 'alarm system' is triggered easily and their thinking abilities disappear into thin air. It happens when they want something that they cannot have or become frustrated with their own inability to do something, or when you request that they do something that they do not like. Depending on their understanding of the situation they may feel that their need for control, security, attention, or to feel successful is not being met.

Little misfortunes such as a balloon disappearing into the air, getting the blue bowl instead of the red one or confusing their times tables create what seems to us an overreaction. When children perceive things as going wrong (remember, children as well as adults act according to how they understand situations, not just according to reality), they find it hard to be reasonable or rational. And, because they are immature, it also takes them longer to calm down.

Emotional reactions

Often, children and adults react emotionally to each other, and their emotions tend to fuel each other's.

Dad is happily reading his paper, while his son is rocking his chair and enjoying his ice-cream. But look what happened!

Something has gone very wrong for the little boy. From his point of view, this is a huge disappointment. Dad has a different perspective on the situation. He knows it is no big deal, and with the best of intentions, he tries to comfort his son.

The boy, however, feels that his dad does not understand. To him, this is a very big deal indeed! He cries even louder to get Dad to see how disappointed he is.

Dad acts according to his own understanding – so much fuss about nothing! And it is all the boy's fault, he shouldn't have rocked his chair in the first place. He is not seeing the boy's perspective, which is quite different.

Dad's stern voice and angry words are more than the boy can take. First, no ice-cream and now Dad is angry. This is just too much! He cries even more loudly.

Dad is taken aback. 'What a mess,' he thinks. People in the café are half-looking, half-pretending to ignore the situation. All Dad wanted was a happy morning out, and look what happened! He is now prepared to buy his son another ice-cream – anything for the sake of getting him to shut up.

Dad's offer comes too late – his son is already in the grip of high emotions and he can hardly understand what his father is saying to him. Soon he will be on the floor, kicking and screaming, not caring about the ice-cream anymore. In fact, he cares about absolutely nothing. He has completely lost it. And Dad now blames the little boy. All this fuss about a stupid ice-cream! 'This child needs a bit of good old-fashioned discipline!' Dad thinks.

What happened here?

In a nutshell – something went wrong for the little boy and his 'alarm system' was triggered. Dad tried to reassure him in the best way he knew but was unsuccessful and so became even more frustrated. Both parent and child became more upset by each other's responses until they ended up on top of 'the mountain of anger'.*

If you have a spirited child, or if you have several children, you may find yourself on the top of this mountain several times every day. This is natural and understandable but also unhelpful and exhausting.

Upset is normal

In the example above, the parent's attempt to stop his child from being disappointed made the situation worse. Dad was trying to stop his son from having his natural feelings, which is not only impossible but also undesirable. Unpleasant feelings are a normal

---

* The 'mountain of anger' metaphor comes from Jan Cox, a systemic therapist and consultant for National Treatment Foster Care.

and healthy reaction to disappointments and frustrations. Being disappointed or upset is a part of life and, while crying and shouting are unpleasant for parents to see, they are a child's normal and healthy mechanism for releasing emotions.

It is not possible for children to be happy all the time and it is not your job as parents always to make things right for them. But you *can* help children to manage their feelings better so that distress subsides more quickly. They may then be able to access the thinking part of their brains again and come up with solutions to their problems themselves. You do this by comforting your children – giving them a hug and a kiss – and using reflective listening (see pages 83–87).

Children speak Childish

Children do not think and speak English as we adults know it. They speak Childish instead – a simple, inaccurate version of English, which is all they know. When their emotions are high, their intelligence is low and their vocabulary becomes even more limited and inaccurate. When parents listen to their children's words as if they were spoken in proper English, they feel unappreciated or even attacked, and often blame their children for being inconsiderate and rude.

A little glossary can come in handy. See if any of the possible translations are relevant to your angry child.

Childish to English glossary

Childish	Possible meanings in English
No. I don't want to. I won't do it You can't make me.	I'm not sure what you want and I'm too embarrassed to ask.
	I know what you want but it seems too hard and I feel I may fail.
	I'm worried or scared about doing it.
	I really don't want to do this because I am tired/hungry/ have other things I want to do.
It's boring.	It's difficult and I'm not sure I can do it.
	I don't see the point of it.
	It is not 'cool' – my friends may look down on me.
	I don't like it.

Childish to English glossary

Childish	Possible meanings in English
It's not fair.	I don't like it.
	Someone else is having something that I feel should be mine.
	You promised this to me and now you are not keeping your promise.
You are so mean.	I'm frustrated with you because you are stopping me from doing what I want.
	I feel that you are winning and I'm losing
I hate you.	I'm so furious that I don't know what to do or say.
	I feel humiliated.
I don't love you anymore! You are not my mum!	I am so frustrated, confused and unhappy, and I don't know what to do or say anymore. I need you to love me whatever I do.

Am I saying that it is okay for children to talk like this? Of course not. We need to teach children to talk in a respectful, mature manner, for their own sake, not just ours. Children need to learn to communicate their needs in English, not Childish!

The way children hear us can also be a problem. When they are angry they do not usually hear our words as we intend them to be heard. Children's understanding of what we say is simplistic, crude, and sometimes completely twisted. They think in Childish.

Things become worse when our body language is less than calm, or when we raise our tone of voice a notch. Children's buttons get pushed. It only takes a nanosecond for their emotions to go up and for their intelligence to go down.

The English to Childish glossary below gives you some ideas about how parents' words are sometimes perceived by their children. Of course, there are many other ways for children to interpret what we say to them. See if any of these may be relevant to you or to your child.

English to Childish glossary

English	Some common translations into Childish
No. Stop it.	Mum wants to control me.
	Mum doesn't understand me.
	Mum doesn't trust that I can do it.
	(*from a child who is used to being shouted at*) Mum is not shouting right now so she doesn't really mean it. I can get away with doing what I want for a bit longer.
You are so naughty.	Dad is right, I am naughty. I can do more bad stuff because this is what naughty children do.
	I am not naughty. Dad is saying it because he doesn't love me.
	I am not naughty. Dad is saying it because he is bad or stupid.
This is unacceptable.	Dad is not happy with me, I'm not sure why.
	I know what I've done wrong – I'm no good.
	Dad doesn't love me.
Stop being so silly.	Mum thinks I'm silly. Silly and stupid are the same. I am stupid.
	Mum doesn't understand me.
How dare you talk to me like this?	Mum doesn't love me any more.
	I'm bad.
You are so wonderful. (*see pages 47–48 for a reminder about the problem with evaluative praise*)	He is only saying this because he is my Dad, I'm not that wonderful really.
	He is only saying this because he doesn't know about the star I drew on the wall under the shelf.
	Dad is saying this because he wants something from me.

Understanding Childish helped me keep calm

'A long and happy day had gone by and it was time for Rob to go to bed. This was the night he was allowed to sleep in my bed but he wanted to bring his giant teddy bear to bed with him. I explained that there was no room for all of us in the bed and suggested that he put the teddy bear near the bedside, but he was having none of this.

'I am a single mum, and this is not the first time that Rob shouted and threatened me: "I will not live with you! I will go to my dad and never see you, not even for one day! Everything we did today was bad! You are so bad!" He was going on and on.

'In the past, I used to get tremendously upset by his outbursts, doubting my ability to be a good mother, but recently I have learned to take things more calmly. Rob is just five, and he speaks Childish. He is simply expressing his frustration.

'The shouts lasted for at least 20 minutes. From time to time, I said to Rob in a calm voice: "You live here. You are going to see Dad on Tuesday." I tried to understand his feelings: "It is hard for you that you cannot have things the way you like." But none of this calmed him down.

'In my desperation, I called a good friend who knows us well. She confirmed to me that Rob did not mean what he said and that he was trying to push my buttons in order to get his way. She also suggested that I did not reply to what he said, as he was not listening anyway, and encouraged me not to give in!

'As soon as I was off the phone, and without any prompting, Rob came to me and said, "Mummy, I'm sorry that I was so nasty to you." I almost cried – I could not believe my ears. I gave him a big hug. He then said "It was completely over me, when I talked to you like that," referring to his anger. I gave him another hug and complimented him for being able to control himself. He fell asleep with a hug and a smile on his face. This was the first time he apologised in this way – I believe he felt he could apologise because I did not shout back at him and just waited it out.

'A few days later something else went wrong for Rob, and he told me again that I was bad and that he was going to go to his dad. I said to him firmly that I did not like listening to this kind of talk and went into the kitchen. This time it only took him two minutes to follow me, give me a kiss and say sorry.

'That same evening, before going to bed, Rob said: "You know Mum, you are *the* leader and I like you." A month has gone by since that incident, without a single threat from him.'

Naomi, mother of five-year-old Rob

You may not say these particular words to your children, but is there anything else that you say that your child may take to mean something you do not intend?

It is wise to teach children to become more mature in their thinking but this can be done only when they are willing to listen. When children are somewhere on the mountain of anger, they are not thinking straight, therefore there is no point in trying to educate them. Teaching children 'English' will need to wait until both of you come off the mountain.

Helping children to manage their feelings

When something goes wrong for children and they get emotional, they need calm, loving adults who can help sort out the problem and offer affection and empathy. Of course, you can give a kiss when they fall over and cry, help to mend their torn artwork or to get a toy that is out of their reach. But it is not always possible or even desirable that you 'fix' everything for your children. Inevitably, sometimes things will not go according to their expectations and they will feel frustration and anger. When this happens, you can help them to manage their feelings better.

When helping children to calm down, you should choose a strategy befitting their 'emotional temperature', or where they are on the mountain of anger.

1 When children are upset, disappointed or sad, but not mad or furious, you can use a skill called *reflective listening*, explained in the following pages. Of course, you can also give them a hug!

2 When children's emotions are higher, they may be far too upset to hear what you say. You will need to use *anger-management strategies*, prepared in advance.

3 On the very top of the mountain, neither of these strategies may work. You may need to *leave the scene*, having first made sure that everybody is safe.

1 Reflective listening

Let's see how Dad could have dealt with the ice-cream accident differently by using reflective listening.

Oh no, the ice-cream is on the floor! Dad now tries to imagine his son's point of view. Although he knows that his son shouldn't have rocked the chair, he realises that now is not the right time to teach his son this lesson.

Understanding how his son is feeling, Dad offers empathy.

The boy is still upset, and Dad is offering more empathy and understanding. Although the boy is still disappointed about the ice-cream, his dad's words help him to feel heard and understood. Instead of getting more and more upset, the boy starts thinking about things he can do to improve the situation.

Dad keeps comforting his son so that the boy feels that his dad is on his side.

No tantrums, shouts or screams!

Does this mean that Dad should get his son another ice-cream? Not necessarily. This is Dad's choice. Whether Dad chooses to buy the ice-cream or not, he can help his son learn not to rock his chair in the future by using the mistakes process explained in Chapter 10 (see page 152).

If Dad does not intend to buy the ice-cream, he would be wise to explain his reasons first and let the boy figure out the 'no' for himself. Dad can say 'Oh no, I haven't got enough money on me' or 'We need to be back home in ten minutes and there is no time to wait in the queue. I know this is hard for you. Maybe we can have something else that you like once we are at home.'

Even if Dad uses all the positive parenting skills, his son may still be upset and Dad must be prepared to deal with his son's disappointment and not to give in, no matter how badly his son behaves. Saying 'no' and then giving in will only teach his son that arguing, shouting and demanding will get him what he wants. If Dad hasn't got the energy to deal with all this, he'd better get the ice-cream straight away.

Reflective listening explained

This is a communication skill for dealing with unpleasant feelings. Reflective listening helps children and adults defuse their emotions, which then increases everyone's capacity to think. When you use reflective listening, your children will feel closer to you, experience your love towards them, and talk and share with you more. Here's how to do it.

- Put your own feelings and critical thoughts aside temporarily.

- Imagine what your children may be thinking and feeling.

- Tell your children what you think they *may* be thinking or feeling. (Don't be assertive or dogmatic about this. You cannot be sure that you are getting it right.) You can also describe what you think your children wish things were like – possibly with humour.

Reflective listening is not about asking questions, explaining, offering solutions, blaming your children or other people. It is also not about agreeing with your children. By reflecting their emotions, you are not necessarily approving their actions. You are making a distinction for them between *having* emotions, which is natural and acceptable, and *acting* on those emotions, which may not be okay.

If you reflect what you think your children may be feeling, and perhaps describe what they wish could happen, they will feel heard, accepted, validated and loved.

Reflective listening has been used by therapists and aware parents and teachers for many years. However, my experience has shown that even parents who know about this skill find it very difficult to put it into practice sometimes.

Because reflective listening requires keeping your own emotions and other agenda aside, it is virtually impossible to do if you are very stressed as a result of your own needs not being met. If you are too angry or exhausted, just don't try it. Give your child a hug if you can, and don't worry. Your child will give you plenty more opportunities to practise reflective listening when you feel better able to do it. And the more you practise this, the easier and more natural it becomes.

Examples of using reflective listening

Your child says:	Give them a hug or put your hand on their shoulder and say:
I hate Miss Jones!	Oh, you probably had a tough time at school today.
Hannah didn't invite me to her birthday party!	Oh, you must be really disappointed.
Can I have a biscuit? Please, please, PLEEEEEASE!	I know you really love biscuits. You wish biscuits were good for you and you could have them whenever you like.
So can I have a biscuit? Please, please, PLEEEEEASE!	*Ask:* Why do you think I'm not letting you have biscuits now, even though I know you love them so much?'
	If children give you a sensible response, praise them: Yes, you gave me the right answer even though it was hard.
	If they say something like, 'Because you are mean', suppress your desire to strangle them! Remember that they speak Childish. Don't let them get a lot of attention for being rude. Instead, say in a calm voice: This is not the right answer. You probably think that I'm mean because you want a biscuit.
	Maintain the reflective listening or just say nothing, especially if they go on pestering you. Do not give the biscuit! This will only teach that nagging and being rude works.
	See Chapters 9 and 10 for strategies to prevent the problem from arising in the first place.
I don't like these potatoes!	Maybe you wish you could have chips every day. You love chips.
	Wait a bit and ask: Why do you think I've baked these potatoes rather than made chips, even though I know you love chips so much?
	Respond as above, according to the answer.
'Waaaaaaaaaah!' *(They are crying and you don't know why.)*	Let me give you a hug. I can see something is wrong.

Getting to the root of the problem

It is natural for young children to become upset when little things go wrong for them. It is also natural for them to feel irritated when you ask them to stop doing what they want to do and do what you ask.

However, if your children experience strong negative emotions over the same issue again and again (for example, every morning not wanting to go to school), this is usually a sign that some need is not being met, or that that is how it seems to them. If they don't want to go to school, they may be experiencing a problem there, such as a teacher being over-critical or another child being rude or aggressive, leaving them feeling stupid or unsafe. It is also possible that they feel the way they do because they misinterpret what is going on around them. They may take a well-intentioned remark from the teacher to mean that the teacher does not like them, or interpret an accidental push by a child as intentional and threatening. In any case, a careful look into the problem is required.

Look how this is done in the example below.

In this situation, you may not immediately think about your child's perspective and needs. Your agenda as a parent is to make sure that your child gets to school on time. You also need to get to work. Understandably, you may instinctively come up with responses like the ones opposite, but they are unlikely to be helpful.

The first response is not useful because it denies what the boy is experiencing right now. The boy, wanting to get his point across, may declare that he hates school and perhaps that he always did. Even though this may not be true, he may then want to defend what he said. So you both end up in a worse place than where you started. The second reply gives the boy information that he already has. He knows he has to go to school; he just wants you to understand that he does not want to.

If Dad understands that his child probably has some negative feelings about going to school, he can choose to use reflective listening. Dad will have a chance to learn what is bothering his son, and they can both think of a plan to deal with it. Because Dad does not know what the reason is, he takes a few guesses.

Notice that the little boy has not immediately agreed or disagreed with Dad, nor has he explained what is upsetting him. But if Dad keeps trying his son will feel more comfortable about saying what the problem is.

Again, an instinctive response is to give advice but since the child has not asked for your advice, he is unlikely to welcome it.

The chances are that the boy will reject his dad's advice, if given, and will tell him that he just does not understand. So instead of giving advice, Dad chooses to continue with the reflective listening.

After giving sympathy and showing his son that he understands him, Dad can ask the boy if he has ideas for dealing with the problem. This will empower the boy to resolve the difficulty himself. The boy will feel more competent and more confident and is much more likely to follow his idea than any advice Dad may give.

Once the little boy comes up with an idea, Dad is quick to praise him for this. The boy now feels proud of thinking up his own plan. The chances are that he will be in a good mood and willing to make up for the lost time by hurrying up a bit.

You may need several attempts at reflective listening in order to get to the root of the problem, just like Dad in the picture, who did not get his first guess right. And, of course, there is no guarantee that your child will open up and share with you what is going on. But when you offer empathy and not criticism, there is a better chance that your child will feel safe enough to talk to you. Even if he does not talk now, he will sense that the communication line is open for him, if he wants to use it.

It takes too much time!

You may think, 'A conversation like this takes so much time! I can't be doing it in the morning. We are all in a big rush. We'll all be late!' From my work with many parents, I have found that the problem is usually not just about time. Arguing with children or dragging them out of bed against their will takes just as long, and sometimes longer!

The difficulty in using reflective listening is usually to do with the stress of managing the morning routine, or the evening routine, the meal, the homework – there are so many things to do and so little time, and it is hard to put your agenda aside and pay attention to every child's individual wants and needs, particularly if you have several children.

If you find that your life is too hectic, it makes sense to allow more time for you and for the children to do things. This usually means reducing your expectations about what you can achieve in any given time. Life with children is slower, especially when you are asking them to do things that are not in their nature. It is best to accept this.

When parents do not take the time to help their children deal with their feelings, everybody ends up angry; children refuse to co-operate and family life becomes a battleground. Inevitably, this is even more so with spirited children, who find it difficult to control their impulses, tend to misunderstand what is happening around them and so often get into trouble.

Can't I just ask what's wrong?

Of course you can just ask your children what is bothering them. Some children respond very well to this and will truthfully share with you what troubles them. If your child is one of these, once you get the reply you can use reflective listening to show that you understand. But many children do not respond well to these kinds of questions – they may just give you a shrug, say they do not know or tell you to go away.

When these children are emotional, they may not know exactly what it is that they are feeling and it is pointless to ask them. At other times, they may know what they feel but may be worried that if they tell you, you will dismiss them or offer unsolicited advice. They may feel under investigation and retreat into themselves even further, to protect themselves from your prying eyes.

So instead of asking, you could make an open-ended reflective-listening statement, such as: 'You look a bit upset, maybe something went wrong for you at school today ...' or 'Some children get really disappointed when they don't get picked for the team, I don't know if it is the same for you ...' – which invites a response. Your child will very likely correct you if your guess is wrong.

Refusing a child's request

Asking questions has already been considered as a way of getting children to do what you ask them instead of what they want, with the least amount of resistance (see pages 63–64). It can be helpful to add reflective listening into the mix.

Here is the little girl who asks to watch TV, but this time things are not so easy for Mum! She starts, as before, asking questions in an attempt to avoid confrontation.

But her daughter's reaction is not what she expected…

Of course, the natural response for Mum is to get upset. If she forgets that her daughter is speaking Childish, her words sound extremely rude and it is easy for Mum to take things personally. In simple English, the girl's angry speech means just 'I'm angry because I want to watch TV'. Without translating into English, Mum's instinctive, though unhelpful, response may be as follows.

If Mum responds in this way, she may feel justified and relieved for a moment or two. But it is almost certain that her daughter will become even angrier, say another thing in Childish and in an instant both Mum and daughter will find themselves on the top of the mountain of anger.

Once translated from Childish to English, the girl's words 'You are really mean' sound more like a cry for help from someone who believes that her needs are not being met. The need behind wanting to watch TV could be to have a sense of control over her life, to relax and have fun, or to belong to her peer group by watching the same TV shows that her friends watch. This does not mean that the girl should be allowed to watch TV, of course, but thinking of her daughter's needs can help Mum understand her daughter's point of view, and not take her Childish words personally. Here is a different response that Mum can make.

Mum may know that this is not true and she may be tempted to contradict her daughter. This will probably lead to an argument, so this is unlikely to be helpful.

Remember – a wise parent avoids an argument at all costs. So instead of contradicting her daughter, Mum can continue to use reflective listening and start to get her daughter to think of the reasons for not watching TV.

The little girl is mature enough to see the reason for herself. Now is the time to praise her descriptively.

Mum's positive attitude helped her daughter find a solution to the TV problem. In a calm moment, later on, Mum can take the opportunity to say, 'Do you remember when you were upset about the TV, and you told me that I was mean? I didn't like that. It hurt my feelings.' It is very likely that her daughter will feel remorseful. She is then more likely to apologise, and genuinely mean it. Mum can also use the mistakes process (see Chapter 10, page 152).

Accepting difficult feelings

'One morning last week there was yet another showdown between my daughter Sophie and our new au pair, Vicky. Sophie was rude again, telling Vicky that she didn't like her and that she wanted her to go away. From the minute that Vicky started to live with us six weeks ago, Sophie has been disrespectful and refused to co-operate with her. I have told Sophie that we all like Vicky and that Sophie will have to accept her. This only made her angrier. I tried to explain to Sophie that her old au pair had had to go back home and that she would come to visit, but this didn't help either. When Sophie was rude, I demanded that she apologise to Vicky but she just refused. All my attempts to reason with her, and my requests that she be polite and considerate whether she liked Vicky or not, were leading nowhere.

'This time, rather than get angry and embarrassed, I decided to bring Sophie and Vicky together. I deliberately sat Sophie on my lap and used some reflective listening, talking about how much we all loved our old au pair, and how much Sophie must be missing her. I said something like, "It is hard to say goodbye to someone you love and have someone you hardly know take her place." After making sure this was okay with Vicky, I also suggested what I thought was one of the reasons that Sophie had a block towards her, this being that Vicky has a deformed thumb. I just said that it is normal to feel a bit uneasy about this, and that people are sometimes different and we can sometimes be embarrassed about it and not know what to do. All three of us spoke openly and very calmly, and I kept on empathising with Sophie.

'The following morning I suggested to my partner that we remain upstairs for longer than normal to see what would happen when the children went down for breakfast with Vicky. Amazingly, it turned out to be the first morning that Sophie and Vicky played very happily together.'

Jane, mother of six-year-old Sophie and two boys aged eight and four

Worries about reflective listening

Many parents worry about reflective listening planting harmful ideas into children's heads. They are concerned that saying something such as 'Perhaps you feel disappointed' may make children believe they should have been disappointed when the idea had never occurred to them. Similarly by saying 'Perhaps you think this is unfair', they are worried that children may think that fairness is an issue when it wasn't before. Fortunately, experience shows that this is very rare. When you get your guesses wrong, children are usually quick to correct you and forget about the whole thing soon afterwards.

To be extra safe with this, when you talk to your children about emotions, you need to be attentive to their responses, particularly to their body language. Children can misinterpret what you say and get confused or scared. Fortunately, they are usually quite transparent and you can usually tell when this happens and put things right.

When reflective listening does not work

When your children are very angry, they may have no brainpower left with which to process your words, however well thought out these might be – what you say will only annoy them. When you or your children are near the top of the anger mountain reflective listening does not usually work. You need to use anger-management strategies.

2 Anger-management strategies

When children are near the top of the mountain of anger, they need something other than words to help them calm down.

- For most children, the easiest route down the mountain is by doing something physical to help release all the stress hormones pumping around their bodies.

- Other children calm down more easily by retreating to a quiet place such as their bed or a hidden corner in the house, perhaps sulking or crying. A little while later, they emerge from there in a much better mood.

- Others get comfort from an object they are attached to, such as a particular blanket or soft toy.

When your children are angry, your first mission is to help them calm down. Only then will they be ready to co-operate, or to learn any lessons that they may need to learn.

When children are in the grip of their emotions, it is not the time to introduce new ideas about handling anger. So, giving them a pillow and suggesting they punch it to 'get their feelings out' does not usually work, if you have never suggested this as a strategy before. You need to find strategies together when you are all in a good mood. Consider the ideas below or create your own strategies and then discuss them together with your children.

Letting it all out

Here are some examples of physical anger-management strategies that children (and some parents) find useful:

- running up and down stairs as many times as possible;

- jumping, dancing or shouting to loud music;

- tearing unneeded paper into strips;

- angrily scribbling on a large sheet of paper;

- jumping on a trampoline;

- hitting a pillow or a specially designed punch bag.

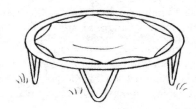

Once you come up with some ideas that seem promising, choose the one which you like most and practise it several times, preferably in different locations in the house.

Sooner or later your children will become angry again. The strategy that you have already practised together will be familiar to them and they will be more likely to use it. If they still refuse to do what you all rehearsed, do not despair. Taming the anger monster takes time and effort. After a few more conversations and a few more rehearsals, your children will be able to remember the strategy and use it even in the heat of the moment.

Parents often ask what to do if their children get angry and they haven't rehearsed an anger-management strategy. My advice is to discuss strategies as soon as they get back home – or as soon as you put this book down. Why wait? Make it your first priority today, and you will have an easier day tomorrow. Invest in your child now, and you will reap the benefits for weeks to come.

Deep breathing and distractions

I'm sure you have heard the advice 'Breathe deeply and count to ten'. When you take a deep breath and count, you are in fact telling your body and mind that there is nothing threatening in your environment and that you can relax.

Even better is to do the following:

- First, after taking a deep breath – it should make your ribcage fill out like a balloon – release the air as slowly as you can. Breathing out more slowly than breathing in brings your blood pressure down, and so helps your body to relax.

- Secondly, do something more demanding of your brain, such as counting backwards from 100, reciting your seven times table or trying to remember the names of all the children who came to your child's birthday party two years ago. You can be creative with the method you come up with – the idea is to keep your brain busy with something that is not trivial but not very taxing either. If you manage to distract yourself from whatever created the upset for at least 20 seconds, the big rush of adrenaline in your body will be reduced significantly, and your angry feelings will lessen too.

As with other anger-management strategies, you need to discuss this when your children are relaxed and practise during minor upsets first. Demonstrate this method yourself while describing what you are doing. Use it during frustrating events that are unconnected with your children, otherwise they may take it personally. Unkind drivers on the road on the way to school, not being able to find your shoes or a leaking carton of milk could all provide opportunities for practice.

Retreating to calm down

If your children already go to their room when upset or reach for their scruffy teddy-bear, they probably don't think of this as a strategy for dealing with emotions. You can help them by explaining that this is exactly what it is – they have already found their own way of dealing with their difficult feelings, which is great!

Instead of interpreting a children's sudden disappearance into their room as an act of defiance or lack of consideration, you can all view it as a healthy strategy to help them calm down, so that they are ready to face whatever it was that created the upset in the first place. Expect them to leave with an attitude – they are angry after all. You can talk about what happened and what needs doing later when everybody is in a better mood.

Self-awareness

Have you ever heard someone bellowing 'I am *not* angry!!!!'? Even adults do not always realise that they are angry when they obviously are, so what hope do children have, unless we teach them otherwise?

It is useful to talk to children about the sensations in their bodies when they experience different feelings. Where in your body do you feel excitement? Fear? Anger? Happiness? Of course, you need to choose a time when your children are relaxed or when they are experiencing a low level of the feeling in question. You can tell your children how you experience different feelings, and explain that different people experience emotions differently.

When people become aware of the build-up of anger in their body, they are in fact learning to recognise their individual 'alarm system'. When you recognise your alarm you will notice yourself starting to climb up the mountain of anger, and you will be able to do something about it before the volcano erupts (such as deep breathing and distractions as described above).

When you teach your children to identify their upsets and other difficult feelings, you are giving them a gift for life. They will be able to recognise their feelings and take appropriate action, rather than get frustrated, resort to misbehaviour or sink into depression.

Hot thoughts and cool thoughts

You have little control over the first thoughts that pop into your head immediately after your 'alarm bell' rings. These thoughts are an automatic response to your fear that your physical or psychological safety is under attack. They are generated automatically without your conscious awareness. Renowned psychologist Martin Seligman calls these thoughts 'hot thoughts'.* The children I work with find this term very intuitive and helpful.

Hot thoughts sound like this:

- 'I will show him, who does he think he is!'

- 'She is doing it to me deliberately!'

- 'How dare he do this to me!'

- 'I'm such an idiot.'

- 'Revenge!'

Hot thoughts are very seductive, leading you straight up the mountain of anger and into trouble. When children (or adults, for that matter) allow themselves to act on their hot thoughts, they may hit people or kick things or reinforce a self-image of themselves as failures.

When hot thoughts pop into your head, they feel absolutely true but they rarely are. They just come into your mind to help you fight a perceived threat to your needs. You experience hot thoughts as if they were real, whereas in fact they arise from

Hot thoughts

'When I'm angry I get hot popcorn thoughts in my head. They pop like popcorn. Sometimes they are true and sometimes they are not.

'My teacher didn't let me answer his questions even though I had my hand up. It happened many times. I got very angry and kept getting hot popcorn thoughts in my head. But I knew I shouldn't believe the hot popcorn thoughts. So after the lesson I asked my teacher why he did not let me speak. He said that he already knew that I know the answers and he wanted to give other children who were more shy a chance. It made me feel much better.'

Eight-year-old David

---

* The concept of 'hot thoughts' together with a technique similar to the 'pizza' were developed and researched by Martin E. P. Seligman (see Recomended reading, page 200).

your individual perception and interpretation of events.

Instead of believing your hot thoughts, you need to challenge them. Could there be another reason why things went wrong? Maybe it is a misunderstanding or an accident? Is there a way to put things right instead of acting on these thoughts? Asking all these questions, and using the pizza technique below, will help you generate cool thoughts instead.

Just as with the other anger-management techniques, it is best to explain hot and cool thoughts in a calm moment. When you teach your child about emotions and body sensations, you can talk about your own hot thoughts and how untrue they usually turn out to be. Use real-life situations to demonstrate this so that when you spot these thoughts, you can all laugh about them. There is no need to take hot thoughts seriously. They are certainly not to be believed before you check them out.

The pizza

The pizza is another tool adapted from Seligman's work, which the families I work with find very helpful. It helps children see that the first hot thoughts that pop into their heads are not necessarily true, and that there could be lots of other explanations for what went wrong.

You first need to draw a pizza and slice it in eight. You then need to choose a story where something annoying happened to the character. The next step is to come up with eight different explanations as to why this misfortune might have happened, and write each explanation inside one slice of the pizza. Some of these reasons can be realistic, and the others can be far-fetched – it is all part of the fun. You then ask your children which reason is true – they will probably realise that it is impossible to know!

Look at the example on the following page: a child asks his friend to join his game but gets no response.

You can use the pizza with your child to help him come up with eight different explanations of what happened:

When you use this technique with children on real-life situations, the first few explanations they provide are likely to be boiling hot! However, once the hot thoughts are on paper and out of the way, cooler thoughts start emerging too.

After you have used the pizza several times, your child will get the idea. The next time things go wrong, you can invite your child to imagine the pizza and think of alternative explanations. Even when your children are too upset to think of explanations for the pizza they may be able to acknowledge that other explanations exist, which in itself can calm them down.

Don't assume the worst

'Peter used to have strong feelings of injustice, say when another child hit him when they were playing rough and tumble games.

'Before we learned about the pizza, Peter would generally assume, and proclaim, that the other child hit him on purpose. The pizza helped Peter understand that there could have been many reasons why he was hit – it could have been that he bumped into the other child's arm, it could have been the child swinging their arm without thinking about where it was going to land, or Peter could have been right and the child might have done it on purpose.

'Using this technique in everyday situations, either about things that happened to him or that happened to us, allowed us to help Peter understand that there are many reasons why things happen, and that we don't always know why. We would play a game in the car, when other drivers were driving badly, to think up as many reasons as possible – they were late and in a hurry, they had only just learned to drive, they'd just been given some really bad news and weren't concentrating, or perhaps they were just bad drivers! It's a fun game, and also helps Peter understand that when we don't know why something has happened, it pays to think about a lot of possible scenarios rather than just assume the worst.'

Mark, father of eight-year-old Peter

In any event, don't expect your anger or your child's anger to disappear in an instant, even if the reason for the anger is now gone. It takes emotions a while to subside. Your bodies need time to readjust.

3 Leave the scene

What can you do if nothing seems to help and your child is out of control? You may have tried to listen to your child's feelings or given your child a hug, or put anger-management strategies into practice to no avail. Or maybe your child's emotions went out of control so suddenly that you barely had the chance to notice that something was going wrong until it was too late. One minute all was fine and the next all hell broke loose.

You may have to accept that there is nothing much you can do in the heat of the moment, and the best option available to you, if you are at home and your child is safe, is to leave the scene until your child calms down.

It is impossible for children to stay on the top of the mountain for ever. Left to themselves, sooner or later, they will come down. Their emotions will subside and their brains will return to normal function. This will be the time for a big hug and for teaching a different way of going about things. Your child dealt with the problem as best he or she could at the time. The most important thing afterwards is not to prove your child wrong and win, but to help your child learn lessons for the future. (Chapters 8 and 10 demonstrate how this can be done.)

Keeping everybody and everything safe

It is not acceptable for children to hurt people or damage property, no matter how they feel. It is especially not okay for your children to hit you, no matter how young or how upset they are. If your children are hitting people or damaging property, physically hold them or move them to a place where they cannot cause harm, being careful not to hurt them while you do so. The calmer you manage to be, the quicker you will regain control. It is best not to talk too much – your words are likely to add fuel to the fire.

No child is too young to be physically stopped from hurting you. I am amazed to see how some parents let their toddlers bite or hit them and excuse this by saying that their child is so young or very upset. When you are stopping your child from hitting you, you are doing your child a favour. In the long run, it is not reassuring for a child to have a parent who is not standing up for him or herself. You need to be quiet, loving and firm, avoiding criticism and blame, yet determined.

There must always be a consequence for hitting adults or for damaging things. The purpose is to teach and to make it up to the person who was hurt rather than to punish. See page 148 for some helpful ideas.

Tantrums in other people's homes or in public places may be especially difficult to handle. On top of the challenge of managing your child, it may also seem as though everyone is looking at and judging you. Difficult as this may be, if you give in to your children they may learn that tantrums work. When a tantrum is in full flow in a public place, there is not much you can do except wait it out, or leave the place with your child, even if he or she is kicking and screaming. (Chapter 8 'Preparing for success' explains how to reduce the risk of tantrums altogether!)

A quick recap

When things go wrong and your child is upset.

If your child is still angry.

If this is not effective either.

Let your children give vent to their feelings, and give comfort when they have calmed down.

Helping your children to deal with their emotions can be extremely difficult. When children are emotional, they often misbehave and can be rude and horrible. You may feel that they do not deserve to be hugged, comforted or listened to. Sometimes you may barely be able to stop yourself from slapping them. However, we are the adults and it is up to us to act our age. Giving comfort does not mean letting our children off the hook. You can and should always come back to and deal with whatever happened, once everyone has calmed down, as detailed in the following chapters.

At such times it can help to remember this wise saying from the American writer Erma Bombeck: 'Your child needs your love the most when he deserves it the least'.

CHAPTER 8

Preparing for success

I expect we have all experienced a scenario like this.

No child likes to stop having fun and go back home because their parent says they should. However frustrating this is for Dad, his little boy is not doing this out of malice – like all children he loves running and climbing and jumping. The swings, slides and other kids in the park attract him like magnets.

Dad is now getting more and more irritated by the minute. There is dinner to be had, emails to check, he may be tired or cold and he just wants to go home. Whether he is aware of it or not, Dad has started climbing his mountain of anger. And the little boy? He has no clue about his dad's agenda. He is far too busy having fun. The boy is doing what is natural for all children to do, which is whatever he likes whenever he likes it!

Not surprisingly, Dad is now even higher up the mountain of anger, feeling more and more upset. From his perspective, his son is being disobedient and disrespectful. Naturally, Dad is concentrating on his own agenda – he feels even more exhausted, hungry and fed up. Now Dad resorts to shouts and threats.

Suddenly, the little boy realises that he is in trouble. 'Dad is really mad at me!' he thinks. His alarm rings loudly and his intelligence is reduced to that of a scared puppy. He still wants to play in the park but he is also dreading his Dad's anger. He reacts in a childish, immature way – by running off.

Now everyone is furious. Dad is blaming his son for not respecting him and threatens punishment. The little boy is wailing, convinced that life is not fair. 'I'm a bad boy and Dad hates me', he thinks in Childish. Everyone loses out.

There is a wonderful way to prevent such upsetting situations from arising and it is called preparing for success. It was developed by learning and behaviour specialist Noël Janis-Norton and it is my favourite parenting skill. It works for me brilliantly in both my personal and professional life.

What is preparing for success?

To prepare for success, you need to take a moment to think about your plans for later in the day and for the next few days and imagine what may go wrong. You can probably predict that your daughter is likely to demand a third bedtime story, that your son may pester you for treats in the supermarket or that he may hit another child at a birthday party that is coming up. You can usually guess what may go wrong – it is probably the same thing that goes wrong time after time. Once you identify what may go wrong, you can prepare your children to deal with it better.

Preparing for success is common sense when you think about it. All of us, adult or child, feel much better when we know what to expect next. Imagine yourself at a train station, not knowing whether the next train to your destination will come in a few minutes, a few hours or maybe not until the next day. How relaxed are you going to be? This is the state of mind in which many children spend their lives – not sure what is going to happen next and when.

Because children cannot meet many of their needs themselves, they are dependent on the adults who care for them. They may worry that something that they don't like may happen, or that they are not going to be able to get something they want. Spirited children tend to worry about this more, whereas easy-going kids usually go with the flow. Whatever their nature, when you tell children what is likely to happen next, they can prepare themselves mentally and get into the right frame of mind for co-operating with you. And the act of preparing them gives them loads of positive attention, which is just what they need.

Thinking ahead may take some getting used to: we don't tend to give much thought to problems before they occur; we usually get reminded of them only when they are on top of us. If either you or your child has recently spent time up the mountain of anger, this is a sure sign that preparing for success can be useful for you.

How to prepare for success

To prepare children for success, ask them leading questions about what is going to happen next, and what they need to do. This is far more effective than telling children what you expect of them. When you ask children what they think is going to happen and how they need to behave, they have to imagine themselves in the future situation and consider for themselves what they need to do. Whereas, when you simply explain to your kids what you want from them they may not pay much attention, or may forget everything you talked about a moment after the conversation is over, or they may feel you are bossing them around.

It is also useful to prepare every night for the next day, even if you do not anticipate particular problems. Just make sure that your children know what the plans are for the day to come. You may be surprised to find out how often they don't, unless you prompt them to remember.

The family management team

The first step in preparing for success is to get the family management team together. Consider the example of the little boy in the previous pages: the boy's parents need to note what happened when he was asked to come home, try to understand his perspective and come up with some practical solutions. Even though Mum was not present at the park, she has probably experienced similar problems at other times. If not, she must be doing something right, and Dad may be able to borrow her ideas! It is best for both parents to agree on a plan to follow so that their son gets one consistent message. Parents need to be realistic about what they expect from their children – calling them just once at the park and expecting them to leave everything behind immediately is probably asking for too much.

When you look more closely at the example on pages 109–111, you can see that Dad repeated his request for his son to leave again and again, but did nothing to enforce it for a long while. Looking at this from the boy's point of view, it is not at all clear when he was expected to obey. Was he supposed to come over to Dad immediately? If so, why did Dad wait for five whole minutes before he called him again? And why did he get yet another five minutes to play after that? Why did Dad snap at him at that particular moment and not a bit later or a bit earlier?

By viewing the world from the child's perspective, the family management team can see that the little boy needs a clearer message that will help him do what he is told. One of the best ways to achieve this is to give him advance warnings.

Advanced warnings are very helpful for kids – they help them to get ready for changes as well as give them opportunities to practise awareness of time. When you keep giving your children one-minute or ten-minute warnings, they gradually learn what these time intervals feel like. Do not hesitate to give such warnings, even if your children have no idea what a particular time interval means just yet. This will help them to learn!

The talk-through

Once you have a good idea of how you want to manage the situation, you need to talk it through with your child or children. In the example on pages 115–122, Dad has the conversation with his son on his own – if two parents are involved, some children may feel that they are being ganged up on. Dad chooses to sit his son on his lap. Having a hug but no eye contact increases affection and reduces confrontation. The talk-through is designed to help the boy change his behaviour for the better in future, not to prove him wrong.

The communication skills covered in Chapters 5, 6 and 7 come in very handy during the talk-through. Dad can descriptively praise good attitude and creative ideas, put aside his own agenda and reflectively listen to the child's frustrations while being affectionate. Above all, he needs to avoid arguments.

When you do this for yourself, expect the conversation to be quite long! A long conversation is a good sign that the child is really thinking about what is being said and that you are covering all the points you need to cover. The time you invest now will be saved later.

First, Dad needs to get his son to be willing to talk to him. One of the best ways to do this is to offer the child limited choice about when to have the conversation.

Dad does not assume that his son would instantly be ready to talk. Instead, by giving him the opportunity to choose, he makes his son feel respected, which immediately puts him in a more co-operative mood.

Dad is probably tempted to say, 'But you said you would talk after dinner!' or 'We have to talk about this whether you like it or not!' but this is likely to lead to an argument and Dad remembers that they will both lose. So Dad finds something to praise and addresses his son's worries about this conversation with some reflective listening and some reassurance.

Now that the little boy is given an opportunity to talk, he comes up with his own grievances, and blames Dad for everything that went wrong.

It is very tempting for Dad to defend himself or to explain to the boy that he got it wrong. But this will lead to a pointless argument, which Dad is keen to avoid. So Dad puts his own agenda aside and tries some reflective listening instead.

Now the boy feels his dad understands him. Needless to say, this does not mean that Dad accepts his son's behaviour. The next stage is to ask a leading question.

Again, it is very tempting for Dad to explain to the boy how important it is for him to have dinner, or to give all the good reasons why they had to go back home. But all this will do is start yet another argument. So Dad just agrees that the boy may not be hungry and persists with his question.

When you ask a child to guess, you are removing some of the risk of getting things wrong. You are in fact saying: 'Think, but if you get it wrong it doesn't matter, it is only a guess.'

Not a great guess, is it? The boy, being childish, is throwing all responsibility back on his Dad. But Dad is more clever – instead of preaching to the boy he agrees with what he says.

The little boy is using all his armour – now it is Josh. Isn't it tempting for Dad to start arguing about whether Josh can stay at the park or not? But again, Dad is more sophisticated than this and he does not rise to the bait. And Dad asks his son a leading question about the park, letting his son figure out the 'no' for himself.

Dad remembers that his child is speaking Childish, not English. 'It's not fair' in Childish probably means 'I don't like it!'. So, instead of arguing about fairness, Dad uses reflective listening.

Because the boy gets sympathy and understanding, not criticism, he is now ready to move on and think about better ways to manage things.

The natural response to this would be 'Five times? You must be joking!' But Dad knows better – he finds something to praise!

What if the boy does not come up with any ideas? In this case, Dad can offer his thoughts, but not before asking his son if he wants to listen. My experience is that when children do not feel threatened they are happy to listen to what you have to say.

The boy really wants to have it his way! Dad lets him have this little victory. And why not?

Dad has enough foresight to prepare for another likely eventuality – that in spite of this long talk-through, his son will not keep to his side of the agreement. This is very important as often children forget their good intentions once they are in the tempting situation. Talking about this possibility in advance makes things much easier.

As you would expect, the little boy is not volunteering consequences for breaking the agreement. He would like to think that all will be fine.

Dad makes sure that if his son gives him trouble, there will be a consequence. The consequence here makes a lot of sense – a delay at the park means less time for a story at bedtime.

This talk-through was not at all easy for Dad. His main challenge was to avoid arguments and confrontations as much as was humanly possible, even though his son kept pushing his buttons. By giving up the natural urge to win and using positive communication skills instead, Dad has helped his son to progress towards being more co-operative. And as with every other life skill, the more you have this kind of conversation with your children, the better you are going to get at it.

If your child is too impatient for this kind of conversation, you can always stop the discussion midway and come back to it later. Preparing for success is about investing time and effort in the short term to reap long-term benefits. And sometimes you need to invest more than you would ideally wish.

A short reminder

Some children have very short memories, especially about things that they do not like. Dad will be wise to remind his son of the new plan just before the next time they go to the park.

Dad asks questions instead of just giving information. This way, he can be sure that the little boy remembers what was discussed. And since the boy has now repeated what he agreed to do, he is more likely to do it.

What if the little boy says he does not remember the agreement? Dad can ask whether he wants a hint. If the boy is in a co-operative state of mind, he will want to please and is likely to say yes. If the boy will *not* co-operate, Dad needs to wait until he does before leaving home. Leaving before that is a recipe for trouble later.

Now Dad asks his son to think about how he will feel when asked to leave the park. To answer this, the little boy needs to imagine himself in the situation, which will help him do the right thing when it comes to the crunch.

Dad ends the conversation on a positive note, using descriptive praise. Will the boy come to his Dad after the two warnings? We don't know. But there is a far better chance that he will.

Shopping

'Shopping with the children was always a nightmare – stressful for me, boring for the kids and an opportunity for them to misbehave. I used to ask Heidi to hold my hand but she kept running away. Oliver used to moan and cry constantly. They both kept asking me for this and for that and would cry when I said no. I felt I was a useless mum and was at the end of my tether.

'Now, before we go shopping, I prepare for success by asking the children to tell me how they need to behave. I also ask Heidi how we can make the trip more exciting for her. She now helps me pick the food, and I let her choose the fruit she will be eating during the week. I praise her descriptively for being so helpful and sensible.

'Both children are allowed to choose one healthy thing such as a banana, which they can hold on to and eat after they leave the shop. It's amazing how shopping has turned into an enjoyable experience for all of us.

Rebecca, mother of five-year-old Heidi and three-year-old Oliver

What should you prepare for?

Prepare for anything that you think could go wrong. Parents I have worked with have found it useful to prepare for any problems associated with daily events such as getting out of bed in the morning, the morning routine, doing homework, eating, participating in household chores and such like. You can also prepare for more special events such as going to a new friend's house, visiting the doctor, eating in a restaurant or going on a family holiday.

How much you will need to prepare depends on your children's age and temperament – some need more preparation than others. Spirited children, of course, need more preparation than easy-going ones.

Many children hate surprises and do not like switching from one activity to another. They hate going to bed and hate getting out of bed. They do not like getting into the bath, but hate coming out, once they are in it. They, more than any other children, need to know what is coming next and when. Having time to adjust helps them feel more secure and puts them in the right state of mind for co-operating with you. Prepare them for everything, from putting on car seat belts to going to visit a friend.

Life-changing events

If your children are facing major life events such as changing school, emigrating to another country, a serious illness in the family or their parents' separation, it is vital that you prepare them as much as you possibly can. Even events that feel exciting or fun to us may be unsettling to our children and are worth preparing for.

You may struggle to cope with such events yourself and find it hard to discuss them with your children. However difficult this is for you, the more age-appropriate information your children have, the more secure they will feel and the easier the transition will be for the whole family. Children need to have a chance to ask their questions and to have you answer as honestly as you can, while protecting them from unnecessary and emotionally disturbing information. They need to feel loved and supported through the transition, and know that any negative aspects of the events are not their fault. Reflective listening (see pages 83–87) is very useful in these conversations.

A father–son chat

'My son joined a rugby club last year, and has practice and games on a Sunday morning. He invariably looks forward to it. I soon became a coach, which I enjoy just as much. The difficulty came when he started whingeing repeatedly and saying, "It's not fair!" when he perceived anything as going against him. I got sharp with him on occasions during training when he repeatedly complained, but this had no effect – in fact, it seemed to fuel the problem. I was casting around for what to do, as it was affecting us both.

'Suddenly I recalled the mountain of anger and a strong image of a volcano came into my mind. When a volcano is erupting, just as when a tantrum is in full flow, it's pretty well impossible to do much about it beyond damage limitation.

'I have now learned that the best time to deal with a problem is when things are quiet and peaceful. I used the 20-minute window we had to ourselves when driving to the grounds, to ask him about things that "weren't fair". And, likewise, tucking him into bed, when he was relaxed, was a great time for a father–son chat. He would mention a boy treading on his foot "on purpose" or someone else being awarded a try "when I hadn't been".

'I encouraged him also to see it from the referee/teacher/parent's point of view. Sure, we sometimes get things wrong, but we do our best. Maybe he himself had once trodden on someone's foot by mistake or scored a try when there was some doubt. He ended up saying how he hated the way a particular Premiership footballer swore and spat. "Rugby players don't do that," he said with some pride.

'Last week there was only a single moan, rather half-hearted. All eyes are now on a tournament in two weeks' time. Maybe it'll be a whinge-free event.'

Fred, father of eight-year-old Michael

A quick recap

Your aim is to help your children be their best in the future, not to prove they were wrong in the past. Preparing for success can help you to achieve this:

- Agree a plan in the family management team.

- Have a talk-through with your children, and be willing to compromise on the details.

- Keep trying to imagine your children's points of view.

- Be affectionate.

- Offer as few explanations as you can get away with – instead, ask leading questions that will make your children think.

- Avoid arguments at all costs.

- Be quick to praise your children descriptively for any contribution they make.

- When your children complain or get upset or angry, respond with reflective listening and reassurance.

- Agree what will happen if your children do not keep to the agreement.

- Give a brief reminder just before the event.

- Don't despair if you don't get immediate success. Think about what went wrong and try again.

CHAPTER 9

Getting your children to want to do the right thing

Even in the most loving families, and even when parents have prepared for success, children sometimes misbehave. Unless you teach them otherwise, even generally well-behaved children will mess about until they are late for school, forget their homework, throw their school bag on the floor as soon as they come home, use rude language when annoyed, sneakily try to spend more time with their latest electronic gadget, leave their towel on the floor after they come out of the bath, leave the dinner table ten times during one meal … the list is endless.

Exasperated parents make many efforts to try to get their children to do what is wanted of them, starting with an explanation of why they are asking and then, if nothing changes, giving a few warnings. Sometimes this can be effective but explanations and warnings often sound like nagging and then children tune them out. Parents then move to the next step of threatening punishment.

Punishments and threats

We usually threaten punishment when we are already somewhere on the mountain of anger and not thinking straight. Sometimes, parents know they have no intention of carrying out the threat and usually the child knows it too. At other times, parents mean what they say but realise shortly afterwards that the threatened punishment is too harsh. One way or the other, children learn not to trust their parents' words. They learn that the threats are empty and therefore that there is no need to pay much attention to them. Then, if the parents finally *do* carry out the threat, the children feel hard done by: 'Dad threatened me so many times, I didn't think he meant it. Why is he suddenly carrying out the threat now?' It is all very confusing for them.

Just like threats, punishments are usually meted out in the heat of the moment, and are often excessive. When children are punished, they feel resentful and sometimes even fearful. At that very moment, at some level, they may even hate their parents. Indeed, many adults today still resent their parents for the punishments they received as children. Other children protect themselves from what seems unfair treatment by distancing themselves from their parents – and may remain emotionally distant as adults. I am not saying that punishments will inevitably destroy your relationship with your children, but wouldn't it be wonderful to have a more positive yet effective alternative?

This chapter will help you tackle whatever challenges you are dealing with right now by using positive means. First, look at the checklist on pages 130–132, to see whether you are using all the positive skills you have learned to maximum effect. Many parents think that they have tried everything when in fact they haven't used even a small fraction of what is available. I used to be one of these parents, too. This is not our fault – very few of us were brought up on positive parenting skills. So how can we be expected to know better?

Using all the positive parenting skills

In order to work out whether you are using all the positive parenting skills that are available to you, think about the particular behaviour you would like your children to change and consider it in the light of the following questions.

Are you using all the positive parenting skills?

Ask yourself...	Possible cause of the problem	How to improve the situation
Are your children feeling physically okay?	Your children may be hungry, tired, restless from lack of exercise or unwell, which makes it difficult for them to do the right thing.	Think about practical steps you can take to deal with this. For example, some children are very hungry at the end of the school day. They feel and behave much better when they get a healthy snack at the school gate.
Do your children understand and remember what will happen next and what they need to do?	Parents often assume that their children understand more than they really do, or that they remember things that were talked about a while ago.	Prepare for success by asking leading questions about what is going to happen, and praising your children's responses. Give a short reminder just before the event.
Are all adults giving the same consistent message to your children?	You may not always agree with your partner about what you want from your children. Or teachers, friends and other family members may give different messages from the message you give.	Get all involved adults to agree – or agree to disagree, in which case you need to explain to your children that they need to behave differently with different people.
Are you getting your point across without telling off, criticising, nagging or shouting?	You may get so upset by your children's behaviour that you lose your temper or become sarcastic, and your children then resist you even more.	Use descriptive praise, avoid arguments and criticism and use non-confrontational language when you ask your children to do what you want.

Ask yourself...	Possible cause of the problem	How to improve the situation
Are you avoiding arguing with your children?	Your children may tempt you into arguments and you may get drawn in without realising it. Then they think that doing what you ask means that you have won and they have lost.	Remember that your aim is to progress, not to win, and that arguments always end up with two losers, so avoid them at any cost.
Is what you are expecting your children to do realistic?	You may sometimes ask for more than your children are capable of doing at their present developmental stage, and get upset when they fail.	Keep your expectations as long-term goals. In the meantime, take little steps towards what you want your children to do. For example, sitting at the table for only two minutes and increasing it gradually.
Are you setting your children a good example?	You may sometimes behave in the very way that you require your children not to behave – shouting, for example – and your children copy you.	You need either to improve your own behaviour or accept that your children will not behave as well as you would like them to.
Are your children bored?	Your children may not find anything interesting to do so they misbehave or bicker with each other.	Create opportunities for your children to play safely whenever possible. Play together when you can, and help them find ways to occupy themselves (see Chapter 12.)
Are you using a lot of descriptive praise when your children are doing things right?	You may be so preoccupied or frustrated that you forget to use descriptive praise.	You need to praise each young child descriptively at least ten times every day – this does not come naturally at first, but it works!

Ask yourself...	Possible cause of the problem	How to improve the situation
Are you praising your children's efforts, not just their achievements?	Your children may find things too difficult and therefore give up.	Praise effort so that your children will be motivated to keep on trying, even if good results are not immediate.
Does your child get enough physical affection?	You may be so exhausted that you don't have enough left to give.	See if you can get help and support so that you can take better care of yourself and your child.
Do you remember to do reflective listening when your children are upset?	You may get so upset by your children's behaviour that you find it difficult to think about their needs and feelings.	Your child is *having* a problem, not *being* a problem! Use reflective listening if you can, and avoid going up the mountain of anger yourself.
Do you have anger-management strategies in place?	You may hope that everything will be okay and forget to teach your children to deal with their anger.	Discuss ways to deal with anger and rehearse them when everybody is in a good mood.
Are you giving all these strategies enough time to work?	You may try things once or twice and when they don't work at once, do something else instead. Out of the best intentions, you may become inconsistent.	Keep on practising all the positive skills even if you don't see immediate results. If you see the value of these ideas and skills and need more support in putting them into practice, try talking to parents who have already done this or joining a parenting class. See pages 202–204 for Useful resources.

Quite a long list, isn't it? Perhaps you can think of even more questions to ask. Identifying what may be missing and taking positive steps to rectify the situation is usually enough to motivate children to improve their behaviour. Parents who go through the list and adjust what they do accordingly are often surprised by how quickly they get results. The problem behaviour may not stop straight away but it is likely to be reduced significantly. Keep using the skills and remember to acknowledge any progress. Once things improve it is easy to forget how bad they used to be.

Learning from their experience

You probably want your children to do things your way out of the best intentions: to protect them from getting into trouble, being unsuccessful in school, being made fun of, losing things or just from being dressed wrongly for the weather.

It must be very tempting for the mum in the picture to insist that her little boy puts his coat on. The trouble is, however, that he may refuse. Even if he complies, he is unlikely to thank his mum for her advice and care. Children want to do what they like. If you insist that they do what you ask, it often ends in tears.

Natural consequences

First of all, you need to consider whether you are willing to let your children experience the natural consequences of their behaviour – being cold because they won't wear their coat, hungry because they won't eat their breakfast, or tired because they won't go to bed – and only insist that children do as they are told if you are not willing to let that happen.

Allowing the natural consequences to occur a few times can save years of power struggles. Your children may be less sensitive to temperature than you think, or are not as hungry as you imagine, or need less sleep than other children their age.

Letting children experience the natural consequences of their actions does not mean that you don't bother to show them how to deal with situations that are difficult for them. You can definitely help your children to become more organised, more competent and more sociable. However, there is not much point in always trying to 'fix' inconveniences for your children. Trying to control what your children do in order to protect them from minor misfortunes often has an effect that you don't intend: you increase conflict and take away your children's opportunity to learn from their experience.

When are natural consequences appropriate?

Many parents have found it useful to let their children deal with the consequences of their actions when they:

- lose toys and other non-essential belongings;

- forget to take their homework, lunch box or swimming gear to school;

- spill or break things accidentally;

- wear the wrong outfit for the weather or for the occasion;

- refuse to eat breakfast;

- are rude to a friend;

- are late to a party or to an after-school activity;

- do not do their homework;

- waste time in the morning and are late for school.

You and your family management team need to decide whether you are willing to let your children face the consequences of certain choices. Fortunately, when you step back and let your children face the music, they often learn to dance!

You may be surprised to see homework and being late to school on the list. Many parents spend a lot of time and considerable effort making sure that their children get to school on time, equipped with all that is required, and that they do their homework well. These parents shield their children from being put in the late book, from explaining to their teacher why they don't have their swimming gear, or from completing their homework during a lunchtime detention.

I am certainly not advocating a neglectful attitude to education. All I am saying is that when children are regularly protected from the consequences that the school thoughtfully puts in place to help them learn, they tend not to develop a sense of responsibility. They happily leave responsibility to Mum and Dad, trusting that they will make everything okay. In the morning, these children may have no idea what time it is, how long it takes to get ready and at what time they need to leave home in order to be at school before the bell. They do not remember what homework they need to prepare and by when, and what equipment they need to take with them on which day of the week. Their parents have unwittingly trained them not to pay much attention to all this. Instead of getting worried about being put in the late book, these kids get annoyed when their parents remind them to stop fiddling with their spoon and eat up their cereal. Not only do parents take the strain, they get no thanks for it. And their children often blame them when something goes wrong.

The best approach is to support a child's learning by establishing clear practice, such as a set morning routine, no TV or internet before homework is complete, preparing school equipment the night before and going to sleep at a reasonable hour. Once such routines are in place, if your children still waste time in the morning or forget their homework, you can allow them to learn from the consequences of their actions.

When you want to help your children to learn from their experience you must let them do what they think is right, without getting annoyed if they choose not to follow your advice, if you have given it. If their decision proves to have undesirable consequences, you can offer comfort without reminding them that they did not follow your suggestion. They already know this! Because you are careful all along to avoid arguments or criticism, children feel less pressure to defend themselves, and may even admit their mistakes.

Dangerous or unacceptable behaviour

Even if, like me, you are a great believer in natural consequences, you are clearly not going to allow your three-year-old daughter to play with fire or your two-year-old son to run into a road. Of course you are going to stop them, and do all you can to prevent this behaviour from ever happening again.

Other childish behaviour, however, lies in the grey area between what we can ignore (letting our children experience the consequences of their actions) and what may put them at risk. Often what your children do is not dangerous but is still not acceptable. Painting on the living room walls, cutting up their new jumper, mixing up Mum's make-up or throwing food on the floor are all exciting activities for kids but usually not acceptable ones. Of course, if you catch your children doing such things, you need to stop them immediately!

Some children obey when you ask them to stop, or even better, stop once they see you approaching. Many others, however, keep doing

I should have listened to your advice…

'The biggest change to our family since learning about the parenting skills is in situations where my children make unwise choices even though I have warned them about the consequences in advance.

'I now show sympathy even when I think my children should have been smarter to start with, and use reflective listening even if I feel like saying things that are far from sympathetic … and I find that they listen to me more as a result.

'For example: Kid goes out of the house without a jacket – I recommend a jacket but he refuses. Hours later he comes back, shivering, cold and miserable. My natural reaction used to be: "I told you to take a jacket, you see, you did not listen to me …" This response used only to put him off and he became grumpy or started arguing with me.

'Now I say: "Oh, you must be so cold, let me cuddle you, let's massage you and get you warm. You must feel miserable." The kid loves the warm response, and feels welcomed at home despite his own misjudgement of the outside temperature. There are no hard feelings, and sometimes I even get the ultimate reward – after warming up a little, he admits: "Oh Mummy, I should have listened to your advice!"'

Sally, mother of four children aged 7 to 16

whatever they like. Their parents end up saying 'no' many times, getting louder and louder, and then shouting, threatening and sometimes smacking. While all this is happening, children are learning that there is no need to listen to parents' first 'no', as plenty more 'no's will follow. Have a look at this example:

Since Dad is not taking any action to stop his son, the little boy is learning that he can continue to ignore him. He may even be secretly enjoying Dad's attention or feeling excited about pushing Dad's boundaries as much as he can.

If your children do not stop what they are doing when you ask them to, don't bother saying anything more than once or twice. It is much more effective to take action – gently take away the pen, the make-up, the food, or remove your children from the place of trouble. Try to distract your children or give them something else to do so that they become less upset. They still may not like it and may complain or cry, but there is not much you can do about this.

Here is what Dad can do:

Since Dad is calm, gentle and uncritical, his son is less likely to make too much fuss about having been moved away from the doorbell. However, some children become unhappy when we stop them no matter how gentle we are. When this happens, it is best to avoid going up the mountain of anger with them, as this is only going to make things worse. No matter how frustrated you are yourself, try to think of your child's misbehaviour as a misguided attempt to meet genuine needs (the child in the picture may need to explore, to play or to control what he does). This will help you keep your own emotions at bay. When you physically stop the misbehaviour, you also limit any potential damage, and there will be less to put right once your child eventually calms down.

Once things are quiet again, you will need to come up with ways to teach your child not to misbehave this way in the future. Just hoping this will not happen again is not enough. Ignoring the bad behaviour hardly ever works – it is too much fun for children to misbehave!

Family rules

But what if problems persist, despite using all the positive parenting skills consistently? You may need to set some family rules. The new rules will state what it is that you expect your children to do, what will happen once they do it (something pleasant or a reward) and what will happen if they do not (something not very pleasant or a consequence).

When you construct your new family rules make sure that it is easy for your children to succeed, and that they will experience the positive side of the rules much more than they experience the negative side. If children's experience of the new family rules is predominantly negative, you may find yourself in a downward spiral of broken rules and escalating consequences, and your children may end up angry and resentful. Setting family rules without using all the positive communication skills, or having rules that are too ambitious, can potentially make things worse. Appropriate family rules provide us with plenty of opportunities to praise and reward our children when they do the right thing. The consequences element of family rules should be minimal. And usually, although not always, the new rewarded behaviour becomes a habit.

Your family rules

You can think of family rules as structures that help everyone in the family have their needs met in a way that reflects your values. For example, rules about eating and table manners meet your need for nutrition, together with your need for a sense of belonging and to give and receive attention. But what you eat and how you eat has got a lot to do with your cultural, perhaps religious, and individual sets of values. There is not one right set of rules about eating that all families should follow. You choose for your own family the rules which are right for you.

If you are raising your kids with a partner, you need to agree your family rules together. This rarely happens automatically – you will need to think together about what you want and how you want to achieve this. Agreeing on rules can be more challenging if you come from different cultures. You may be living with your partner in his or her country, where the culture is different from your own, or you may have both come to live in a place which has different rules from the ones you were brought up with. This is where creative thinking is called for: designing rules that reflect your values and sit well with the demands of the society around you.

Family rules are in fact rules for *parents*, not for children, and for this reason you should use them as a last resort. You cannot control what your children do, no matter how many rules you establish – they may do what you ask or they may not. You can only control your own responses to your children's actions. So it is *you* who has to follow through on the rules even when you are tired or preoccupied and your children nag, whinge or beg you to change your mind. Unless you have made an obvious mistake, you need to keep the rule in place for at least a month otherwise you risk being inconsistent. It is very easy to make up rules and think of pleasant rewards and unpleasant consequences but it is far more difficult to follow through on them day after day.

An example of a simple family rule is: all family members must put their plates in the dishwasher after each meal. Once children do this, they are free to go and play. However, if they leave the dining area while their plates are still on the table they will need to put two additional items in the dishwasher. This kind of rule works with children who are co-operative but forgetful. The parents will need to call them back to the dining table to clear their plates if they have not done so already, and make sure that they take the consequence of clearing another two items. So the rule is, in fact, for the parents to follow.

Before you set your rules, you need to consider what your children are – and aren't yet – capable of doing. Then aim for a rule requiring them to do only slightly more than they are doing already. As they become more proficient at putting their shoes away, laying the table or whatever it is that the rule relates to, you will be able slowly to raise the bar further.

Involving your children

If your children are very young, you can agree on family rules without involving them in the decision. The older your children are, however, the more they need to be involved in shaping the rules. The aim is to help everyone in the family to be happier than they are now – it is not just about getting your children to toe the line.

First, think about a way forward with your family management team. Then, have a discussion with your children and bring to it an open mind, not an empty mind! Present the problem to your children, ask them how they think you can solve it, and write down all their ideas, even the outrageous ones. Add your ideas to the list. Then discuss each idea separately, thinking about whether it would or wouldn't work and how you could modify it so that it might. Only then choose the one you all like the most.

Don't discount any idea – often the very silly ones can be modified and made usable. Many families have been surprised by their children's creative thinking, imagination and good will, once they are given the chance to participate in solving problems!

Writing it down

Once you agree on a family rule, get together to put in writing the action that has been agreed on and what will happen if it isn't carried out. Have everyone sign it and then display the written agreement where everyone can see it. Otherwise you may forget what you agreed and all your effort will have been in vain. You can use pictures for children who are too young to read. This will help you all to remember and stick to your agreement.

KITCHEN CLEANING ROTA

* Monday: Tom
* Tuesday: Emily
* Wednesday: Emily
* Thursday: Parents
* Friday: Tom
* Saturday: Parents
* Sunday: Parents

Computer turned on ONLY when kitchen is clean – Mum to inspect.
Children get ① reminder – if job still isn't done, kids will have to clean extra day instead of parents.

Signed: Mum DAD Tom Emily

Being specific

Make sure that your new rules state exactly what you would like your children to do. Statements such as 'Behave well' or 'Be kind to your little brother' are not specific enough and are open to interpretation. After all the effort you put into constructing the new rules, you may end up arguing with your children about whether or not their behaviour was up to scratch. It is far better to define your rules in specific terms, such as 'Staying in bed all night', 'No hitting or kicking' or 'Getting dressed all by yourself'.

Rewards

It is much easier for children to do something difficult or boring if something enjoyable happens immediately afterwards, so it makes sense to plan the family daily routine accordingly. Here are some ideas families find useful:

- Agree on a morning routine that requires your children to get dressed before they can have their breakfast, so that breakfast motivates them to get dressed.

- If they finish breakfast early, make sure that they can play a game or do something else that they like – this will encourage them to speed up their whole morning routine.

- In the evening, establish that homework and other chores have to be done before children can attach themselves to their favourite electronic gadget. If the homework is not finished on time, some electronic time may be lost. This solves the seemingly never-ending problem of trying to drag children away from the TV and computers to do what they have to do.

All children are different so they are motivated by different things. But almost all children can be motivated by even a few minutes of a parent's undivided fun time and positive attention. Playing a short game together, an extra story, a slightly later bedtime, spending a few minutes with you in your bed in the morning or having a pillow-fight are all good rewards for kids. Why not ask your children what will motivate them? This will ensure that the rewards you are giving are meaningful to them.

Rewards should be as closely related to the event as possible. It's best to avoid using food, especially sweets, as rewards. This is because children can learn to associate food treats with being

Ready for school

'My seven-year-old son has a Game Boy, which, inevitably, he loves to play with. Getting him to do anything was always an effort, but the most stressful times were in the mornings, as I had four other kids to ferry to various schools too. I resorted to nagging, shouting, then physically having to help him get ready and manoeuvre him into the car.

'After learning about parenting skills, I realised that he did not clearly understand his morning routine and what was expected of him, as I had always tended to his every need just because I felt I had to, so as not to let my other kids down. In addition, I realised that, if the Game Boy was somehow used as a reward for completing the morning routine, this would egg him on not only to get ready for school but also to get ready faster!

'So now my son knows his morning routine – we talked it through step by step. He also knows that if he finishes his routine with time to spare, including doing some piano practice, he can have time on the Game Boy. So, when he finishes his routine in good time, we're all much happier! If he doesn't, there is no Game Boy time in the morning at all. The very toy that caused us so many problems has now become the carrot for him to be more independent and do some extra work!'

Helen, mother of five children aged 7 to 15

approved of, which can encourage a 'comfort eating' habit later in their life.

You may sometimes want to use material rewards to motivate your children. However, unless you are willing to risk raising a little tyrant who demands payment before doing anything you ask, these occasions should be rare.

When your child follows the new rule, you have a perfect opportunity for appreciation and descriptive praise. Children need to feel successful and want to be good; keeping to family rules can be an excellent way to succeed and be appreciated.

Star charts

When teaching young children new habits, you can agree on specific goals and reward success with stickers. Parents often use star charts successfully for creating habits such as using polite language, performing household chores, sitting down to do homework without arguments and staying in bed at night. A page full of stars is often all that is needed. At other times, you may wish to give your children non-material rewards, such as some special extra time with you. This is often more fun and more motivating than presents you buy.

Before you start with the chart, both you and your children need to know exactly what behaviours will be rewarded by stars and what behaviours will not earn any. It is best to make it easy for your children to earn stars so that they can earn more than a few every day, and the chart quickly looks cheerful. They should also have the chance to earn a star even if their behaviour is not perfect. Whenever you give a star to a child, remember to be generous with your descriptive praise!

Here is a star chart created for a child who is clingy and anxious about doing things by himself. Note that the behaviours that earn him stars are specific so it is easy to know whether he deserves a star or not. He is rewarded for small achievements – each two minutes by himself earn him a star.

Jonathan is learning to be more independent!

Tuesday 6th June

* I played by myself for ② minutes ☆☆☆☆☆☆☆
* I got something from my room on my own ☆☆☆☆☆
* I said goodbye to Mummy without crying ☆☆
* I stayed quietly in my bed all night

Once a star is earned, it should never be taken back no matter how badly your child behaves. You can deal with the misbehaviour in other ways. If you take stars away, you are opening the door to endless pleading and negotiations.

Star chart worked wonders

'My wife Penny starts her work early in the morning, so managing the morning routine is my job. Getting three children ready for school so that I can go to work is quite a task, which used to be a big source of stress and tension for us all.

'When we started using the new parenting skills, the two older boys were nearly self-sufficient but Toby, my youngest, kept playing up. He would get up, head straight for the television downstairs and plant himself in front of it. I would tell him that I was going to make his breakfast and what it was. If he was in a bad mood then the battle started from there. If he didn't like what I suggested, he insisted he wouldn't eat it. Once we agreed on what he should eat, he would want to have it in front of the television. I would ask him nicely to come and eat his breakfast at the kitchen table but this rarely worked. I would then ask several times – each time getting louder and more cross. I tried everything that I could think of to deal with this – ignoring his bad behaviour and changing the subject, or just shouting at him – which only got him to shout back. He would also dig his heels in on the rest of the routine and I would end up running around after him to find his uniform, pack his bag, pick up his violin, put his socks on, etc.

'We would end up leaving the house late – the other two boys would be late to school and I would be late for work. The whole atmosphere was very tense and we would all start the day in a fairly negative way.

'After taking advice, we have realised that Penny needed to take part in establishing the morning routine even though she is not usually there. We discussed together what we wanted to change about Toby's behaviour, and made a chart with the specific behaviours that we wanted to see. We brainstormed some ideas for non-material rewards for Toby and came up with ideas such as 15 minutes to play a game with Mum or Dad, making cakes with Mum, going on a bike ride with Dad. We then sat down with him, explained how the chart would work and asked him what rewards he would like. He chose to go for a bike ride with me at the weekend.

'We had tried star charts a few times before – usually our intentions were good, but after a few days, the enthusiasm waned and we would revert to previous habits. The rewards we set usually involved buying something so it was also quite expensive! This time, though, our expectations were very clear, Toby had a say in structuring the chart, and the rewards involved quality time with us. We also made sure that he got opportunities to get plenty of stars, and that with every star came a phrase of descriptive praise. Most importantly, we agreed to keep going and be consistent about it, even if we didn't see immediate results.

'Toby now gets up, makes his bed, opens his curtains and gets dressed every morning, including weekends, and the star chart is not needed any more. We are still careful to use plenty of descriptive praise though!'

Adrian, father of two teenagers and seven-year-old Toby

Consequences

When you discuss your new family rules you need to put appropriate consequences in place as well as rewards. Be creative and try to come up with consequences that are constructive, rather than punishments for the sake of making your children feel bad.

As mentioned, the best consequences are natural – they are just what follow as a result of a particular course of action. (If you don't eat your breakfast, you will be hungry later in the day.) When you build your home routines with rewards to motivate your children to do the right thing, the natural consequence of them not following the routine is that they will not be able to enjoy the reward.

At times, however, natural consequences don't work as a solution. For instance, you may wish to teach your children to tidy up their toys, and although the natural consequence of not doing so is a messy room that won't bother them!

In such cases you need to give your own consequences. For these to be effective they need to be small and immediate. Small consequences are easier to enforce without too much hesitation. When you threaten a big consequence, such as missing a party or an outing, you are often reluctant to follow through. You may ignore the bad behaviour or make excuses for your children because you don't want them to miss out and because you know that if you follow through your children will take it very badly. So you wait and wait while your emotions escalate, and at some point you snap.

Another trouble with big consequences is that once they are enforced, you may have nothing much left to motivate your children with. 'No internet access for a month!' you declare. And your children feel that there is no point in trying to please you because they have already lost everything that is important to them, so their mood and behaviour go downhill.

If you have agreed in advance or have at least informed your children about small consequences, you don't feel so bad about enforcing them and have a better chance of stopping the problem behaviour before it gets out of hand.

Consequences should be enforced as soon as possible after a rule has been broken and be closely related to it. This makes it easier for the child to connect the consequence to the offence, and it helps you all put the unfortunate event behind you quickly and move on. A child who has a consequence looming in a few days' time may spend these days sulking, trying to argue about it or refusing to co-operate.

When you enforce consequences, be neutral, or even empathetic in your tone of voice. The consequence in itself is difficult enough for the child – there is no need to be angry about it as well.

Try not to create a situation in which you are giving more than just a few consequences or you may get into a negative cycle. Aim for 90 per cent rewards and 10 per cent consequences. You want your children to experience success rather than failure. You certainly don't want them to feel hard done by and decide that there is not much point in trying. If you have taken into account what your children are capable of doing before setting the rule, there is less risk of the rule being too ambitious and your child constantly failing.

Examples of family rules

Here are some rules and consequences that families have found useful:

- Any toy or plaything left on the floor overnight will be taken away until your children do something for you in return for getting it back. You can use this as an opportunity to get your children to do something constructive, such as helping you with household chores. A rule like this can change your attitude to tidying up after your children: you and they know that they will have to work to get their item back and so you won't feel like a slave! It is also much more meaningful than threatening to throw the toy away. Since you picked up the toys, they have to do something for you in return. No hard feelings.

- If your children use language that you don't consider appropriate, you can have a swear box and make them put a small but not insignificant amount of money in it every time they swear. If they refuse, you can simply take it out of their pocket money. It is, of course, only fair that if you yourself swear, you pay an equally meaningful sum into the swear box!

Ideas for appropriate consequences

- If children leave things lying around or create a mess, the consequences could be one of the following:
  - washing a pot;
  - emptying the dishwasher;
  - cleaning the dining table;
  - feeding or cleaning up after your pets;
  - tidying away a certain number of items.

- For pushing or hitting a parent or being rude, depending on severity, an appropriate consequence could be some way of making it up to this person, such as:
  - preparing something for them to eat;
  - writing a note of apology or drawing a picture;
  - performing little services such as fetching items from another room;
  - making a cup of tea;
  - washing their car;
  - massaging their shoulders.

- For lack of co-operation, the consequence could be:
  - losing a few minutes of an enjoyable activity (rather than losing it all);
  - putting money into a charity box;
  - holding a parent's hand, or sitting next to the parent for a few minutes, instead of being free to play, when the misbehaviour has occurred in a park or other public place.

Time out and the naughty step

For those who don't know, these two techniques are about making misbehaving children stay in their room or sit on a particular step for a set period of time, determined by their age – three minutes if the child is three, four minutes if the child is four and so on. Each time the technique is used, the parent needs to explain beforehand the reason for the punishment.

I find that a lot of parents who come to me for advice have tried to use these techniques in the past, but that not so many actually find them helpful. If you are using these techniques and you feel they work well for you, I wouldn't suggest you stop. Parenting is hard and anything that can bring peace and quiet to our lives may have its place.

The trouble with these techniques is that often children are too upset to listen to their parents' explanations, or they run off, or trash their rooms while in there, or sit on the step for the required time and then continue to misbehave. Sometimes children do stop the misbehaviour but feel extremely resentful or deeply insulted. A parent recently told me that her five-year-old son now refuses to talk to his grandparents because he was so hurt by being made to sit on the naughty step. It came as a total shock to him and weeks after the event he has not got over it.

When children seriously misbehave, trashing property and hitting people, these techniques are unlikely to be effective because the children are unlikely to comply. It is far better to stop them physically – take them away from the place of trouble or hold them so that they can do no more harm, making sure you are not hurting them. Holding children tells them that their bad behaviour and high emotions are contained and that makes them feel safe, because out-of-control emotions are frightening to them too. Isolating them in a room may give the message that you are fed up and just want them to be away from you. It also denies two of their most important needs – to be accepted and to belong.

My hope is that you will get sufficient positive skills from this book to render these techniques unnecessary. And that if your children need to be separated from you for a while because their behaviour is unacceptable, they will go to their room as part of an anger-management strategy that you have agreed with them, not as a form of punishment.

One step at a time

Some years ago, we sat down as a family and wrote a whole page of what we thought were to be our new family rules. Children were to help more in the kitchen, go to bed when told, get up as soon as we woke them in the morning, get ready for school without any fuss, do their homework, practise their instruments every day and so on.

Predictably, none of these things actually happened! These weren't family rules. They were an unabridged list of parental fantasies, to which our kids politely agreed. We had put in nothing to motivate our children to do what we asked and had no consequences in place. We did not consider the need to follow through either. We just had this ideal of a perfect family in mind, where everything goes smoothly and no one ever gets upset. A few days later we came back to reality and decided to work on just one problem area – the morning routine. It took months to crack.

To get results we had to make several changes – no single step was effective on its own. First, we did our best to make sure the children all went to bed earlier. We prepared them for success in the evenings by discussing what will happen the next day and making sure that they had all the equipment they needed for school. However much I hated it, I started getting up earlier myself – this helped me to reduce my own stress levels in the morning. And, most importantly, we set an exact time for leaving, and the children got ten- and five-minute warnings. Any child who was not ready in time had to skip some or all of their breakfast. Our mornings never became idyllic – I guess we not are morning people – but they were far better than before.

A quick recap

If your children are not behaving well yet:

- see if you can take a step back and let them learn from their experiences;
- look at the checklist on pages 130–32 to make sure that you are using all the positive skills consistently.

If this is not enough:

- agree with your partner what you would like to achieve and how to go about it;
- involve your children in creating a new family rule;
- define what they are expected to do in specific terms;
- make sure it is easy for them to succeed;
- agree appropriate rewards and consequences, preferably built into your routine;
- write the new rule down on paper and put it on the wall;
- follow through – stick to your plan.

Do not underestimate the importance of that last point. When you are considering a new family rule, think carefully about whether you are willing to follow through on it, day in, day out, no matter how you feel, without giving in, forgetting or diverting from it. When you make a new rule but fail to follow through on it, children learn that they cannot trust what you say. They figure out that if they persist you will give in. Next time they want to have their way, they will use all their tricks and press your buttons even harder until you blow up. If you are not sure that you are able to follow through, concentrate on using the other positive parenting skills described in this book to deal with problems. They do work.

CHAPTER 10

Learning from mistakes

When children break something, are rude or hurt someone, whether it was intentional or not, they may apologise of their own accord and want to put things right. If so, all you need to do is give them a big hug, praise them for being so grown-up, forgive and move on! However, at other times, children are slow to say sorry and our instinct then is to demand an immediate apology. But children may feel humiliated by this, or may still be angry and refuse. Even when they do say sorry, it often sounds like this:

When children respond in this way, it is usually because they do not feel at all sorry. As far as the girl in the picture is concerned, she hasn't done much wrong – in her view Mum tried to make her eat something disgusting and then overreacted to having a little bit of food touch her sleeve. Being immature, children are absorbed in their own world and find it hard to understand the impact of their words and actions on others.

By asking your children to say sorry when they are not, you are in fact asking them to lie. You are using your power over them to make them say what you want, even when they do not mean it. The ladder cartoon on page 40 shows how this may feel to the child. Apologising may become connected with losing a battle, and not admitting responsibility becomes a matter of pride. Do you know adults who find it almost impossible to own up to their mistakes? They may go out of their way to be kind to you when they hurt you unintentionally, but they will not apologise, no matter what they have done. Not being able to apologise can create huge problems in relationships or at work later in life. This attitude usually starts during childhood when apologising was associated with being humiliated.

When you think of behaviour in terms of right and wrong, good or bad, your children feel judged. They may also worry about being punished if their behaviour is deemed bad. The temptation to defend themselves by denying responsibility, lying or blaming others is huge. They may lie even when the evidence is clearly against them.

Wouldn't it be much better to help your children think about what happened, consider the impact of their words or actions on other people, feel remorseful, make it up to the people they hurt and apologise because they really want to? To help you do this, you need to take a different perspective.

Misbehaviours are mistakes

Some behaviours are clearly mistakes – children may leave their PE kit at school, spill their morning cereal or get their maths wrong. This kind of mishap is the easiest for both parents and children to handle – even if it is caused by forgetfulness, clumsiness or not doing their best, it is an unintentional slip, a mistake, not a deliberate act.

At other times, children know they shouldn't be doing what they are doing, yet they do it anyway. They act on impulse, usually when parents are not looking – snatching toys from each other, making a tower of kitchen chairs to reach a secret stash of sweets they are not allowed to have, or spilling paint over the living room carpet even though they know they must paint only in the kitchen. Although such behaviours can be deliberate, I suggest that we think of these as mistakes as well. This is not how most people think about it – I will explain why I think this is important in the next paragraphs.

When our children do something that they shouldn't, perhaps even causing damage or putting themselves in danger, we instinctively wish to punish them. In our anger, we want to do something that will hurt our children and teach them a lesson that they will not forget. Many of us believe that punishments help children learn – after all, this is how most of us were brought up. Children do learn from punishment, but often they learn a very different lesson from the one we intend to teach. They may learn to be even sneakier to avoid being caught, to lie and deny responsibility for their blunder or to blame others for it. Justifiably or not, they usually feel hard done by and blame everybody but themselves.

Punishment does get children to improve their behaviour sometimes, which is why some parents use it. But this usually comes with a heavy price – children's motivation is fear, not understanding, and they may hold huge resentment towards their parents for years to come. Many adults who were punished as children still resent their parents emotionally, even though intellectually they understand that their parents did the best they could at the time.

If punishment is not a good choice, does this mean that we are supposed to ignore what the child has done, stand by and do nothing? Not at all. Children need to deal with the consequences of their actions and learn how to improve for the future. This is usually much more difficult for them than accepting a punishment, because they are required to reflect on their actions and take responsibility for the effect these actions had on people around them. Most children's mistakes are impulsive, and they regret them immediately after the event. They do not want to be made to think about what they did. They just want the incident to disappear. The mistake process, detailed in the next pages, is not at all an easy option.

When you define 'bad' behaviour in neutral terms as mistakes, it becomes much easier for your children to admit that they could have done better. If they do not fear punishment they are more open to putting things right and learning from their mistakes. As a result, they learn to develop a more mature attitude towards mistakes and imperfections – their own and those of others.

The boy in the picture denies responsibility for breaking the picture frame even though it is obviously clear that he played football in the living room. The mistakes process demonstrated on the next pages will show you how his mother can help him take responsibility for his actions, deal with the consequences and learn a useful lesson for the future.

Responsibility is shared

When things go wrong between people, responsibility is almost always shared, although not necessarily equally. One person may be more responsible than the other for whatever went wrong, but it is very rare that one person holds full responsibility while the other has none.

Think back to the ice-cream scenario on pages 74–76. The little boy definitely made a mistake by rocking his chair and dropping the ice-cream. But his father made mistakes too: he failed to see what happened from his child's perspective and was quick to lose his patience. Who was responsible for the tantrum? I think both parent and child.

The food incident at the beginning of this chapter (page 152) shows shared responsibility as well. Of course, the girl shouldn't have thrown her food at her mum, no matter how much she hates broccoli. But did Mum have to insist that the girl eats it all? And was it wise of her to demand an apology before her daughter was ready for it? Probably not.

The mistakes process

I learned the mistakes process at The New Learning Centre (see Parenting courses, page 204). It is a simple four-step plan to deal with mistakes, which is put into action after the immediate crisis is dealt with and once we are no longer at the top of our anger mountain. The process helps us learn from our mistakes while minimising the risk of negative emotions escalating again. It can also help us to keep our calm when a problem is occurring, knowing that we can deal with it effectively later.

The four steps of the process are:

1 admitting the mistake;

2 making amends/apologising;

3 learning for the future;

4 forgiving everybody and moving on.

1 Admitting the mistake

Start by admitting your own mistake, even if it is not nearly as bad as your child's. When children see us readily admitting our own mistakes, they learn that mistakes are no big deal and admitting them is normal. It makes it easier for them to take responsibility for their own actions.

Make sure you deal with just one mistake at a time. Bringing in more mistakes as you go along may create resentment and prevent you from moving forward.

Of course, Mum in the cartoon on page 155 is not responsible for her son playing football in the living room and it is completely understandable if her first reaction to the broken picture frame is to scream. And she may, or may not, want to clear up the glass before talking to her son. But once Mum calms down, she can think of her own contribution to the situation.

We are going to do the mistake process. My mistake was that I didn't make sure you had a chance to play in the park after school, so it was really hard to keep away from your football. What do you think your mistake was?

If her son gives her a sensible reply, Mum needs to acknowledge it with a lot of descriptive praise. If you do not praise your children for admitting their mistakes, they will find it more difficult to own up to their mistakes in the future.

The child may not admit his mistake and may continue to claim that he did not do it. If this happens, Mum will be wise to make sure that her son does not think she believes his denial. Instead, she can say: 'I know you played football in the room and I am sure you did not mean to break anything. I hope you will tell me the truth when you are ready. I will not be cross with you when you tell me the truth. I will be proud of you for being honest. I know it is not easy to admit you made a mistake after you said you did not do it.' If her son still does not admit the mistake, Mum can ask at a later time: 'Are you ready to tell the truth now? I will be proud of you when you do.'

No matter how much we try, there is no way to make sure children always admit their mistakes. Believing we can control what children say or do is an illusion. Fortunately, we can help our kids become more and more honest by making it easier for them to tell the truth.

2 Making amends/apologising

The next step is to fix whatever was broken and/or to apologise to the person who was hurt. Putting things right again will also help everyone reduce their anger or guilt.

The boy in the cartoon may need to pay for what he broke. He and Mum might go together to the local frame shop, see how much it will cost to replace the glass and think about him paying for at least part of the damage. If the boy hasn't got enough money, he can do some jobs at home to earn it. Rather than punish her son, Mum helps him put things right. There is no need for Mum to get angry with him at this stage. Dealing with the consequences of the mistake is difficult enough for him.

If a person was hurt as a result of a child's action, the child may need to apologise, and perhaps do something for the person to make up for the hurt caused. The same applies if the child is rude and hurts someone's feelings. You may wish to consider Ideas for appropriate consequences on page 148.

If you, as a parent, make a mistake, it is only fair that you apologise for your part too.

3 Learning for the future

Once you have dealt with the consequences of the mistake, it is good to use what happened as an opportunity for learning how not to make similar mistakes in the future.

Mum remembered to praise her son for his suggestion. If her son does not come up with a sensible suggestion, Mum can give her own ideas. It is best to present these ideas as ways to avoid future mistakes rather than as punishments. Mum may want to create a new family rule about keeping the football in the shed, write it down and put it out for everyone to see.

The learning step of the mistakes process can also be used for practising appropriate words children can say to express their angry feelings. If your children were rude to you while angry, remember that they were speaking Childish! Help them think of acceptable words they can say or even shout, such as 'I'm mad! I'm furious! It's not fair!' When children learn to start with the word 'I' and avoid using the word 'you', they will be able to express their anger and frustration without offending others.

4 Forgiving everybody and moving on

Once the lessons from the mistake have been learned, it can be put behind you. The matter is closed – there is no need to mention it any more. Going over it all again will only make children feel resentful or damage their self-esteem. It is best to move on. Much later, you may even laugh together about what happened and about yourselves – many mistakes are quite funny in hindsight!

Mistakes at work

'After learning about the mistake process, it dawned on me how differently I manage my work environment from my family life.

'At work I am responsible for the computing environment – networking, servers and such like. Whenever an incident happens that causes disruption to our users, we have an established and stringent process of "lessons learned": we fix the problem as a first priority, then check what went wrong and finally examine what we need to put in place to prevent such an incident from happening again. Ignoring the incident is not an option.

'Yet at home, when my sons misbehave or cause trouble, I am completely at a loss. I "shoot from the hip" – sometimes ignoring their behaviour hoping it will stop, sometimes threatening them (with no apparent affect) or punishing them, only to have my wife chastise me for being too harsh. And then I try to forget all about it.

'My family is infinitely more important to me than my work – it now seems completely crazy that I used to ignore problems before. The mistakes process gives me and my wife a clear action plan, with which we are both comfortable.'

Steve, father of two boys aged eight and eleven

Introducing the mistakes process

It is always best to introduce new ideas at a calm moment. When you have some time, explain the four steps to your children, using examples from your own life. For instance you might say:

'Do you remember the mistake I made yesterday when we went to the shop and I found I had left my money at home? Now, the first step in the process is to admit my mistake, which I just did. Then I need to apologise to you, because we couldn't buy the milk and had to come home and go to the shop again, and all this time you were hungry and tired. The third step is about the lessons I need to learn – I must check that I have money on me whenever I leave home to go shopping. And the fourth step is to move on and not feel bad about it any more. I think I can do that.'

You can demonstrate the process further with stories that you read or make up, discussing the characters' mistakes and imagining what the mistakes process could be like, if they carried it out.

Will it cause upset?

When things have gone wrong and you finally manage to calm everyone down, usually the last thing you want to do is to talk to your children about what happened. Understandably, you want to forget about the whole incident and hope that it will never happen again. You may be worried that raising the issue will bring back bad feelings and start up the shouting and arguments.

This is unlikely to happen when you use the mistakes process because you concentrate on making things better, not on making your children feel bad. Children usually have mixed feelings about their mistakes. On the one hand, they feel guilty about what they did and want to put things right – they want to appear good in their own eyes as well as in yours. On the other hand, they worry that their mistakes will show them to be stupid, bad or complete failures. They may also suspect that others (such as you or their siblings) will bring up whatever it was that they did, and they may be made to feel wrong, excluded or not good enough.

The mistakes process avoids all this by giving both children and adults a chance to make amends and learn without losing face. Once the process is completed, everyone is relieved and the children feel at peace with themselves, knowing that all is forgiven. There are no hard feelings and everyone can move on from the unfortunate incident.

When other people are around

Most people are not familiar with the mistakes process and will expect you to demand that your children apologise immediately, for example when they have pushed or hit another child. You can ask your children what it is that they have to say, and if they apologise readily, then all is well. Don't forget to praise them for this! However, if they refuse to apologise, believing that they are right and the other child is wrong, explain to the people around you that you are taking matters very seriously and that you are going to have a long discussion about what happened when you are back home. You can add that you intend to make sure that your child appreciates what they have done and understands the need for an apology. When you get home, embark on the mistakes process. Your children can apologise later if need be.

When children bicker and fight, be careful to not apportion blame unless you are absolutely certain about what happened. It is best to keep out of children's bickering as much as possible but instead allow them to sort out their own disputes. Remember that children are not mini-adults! Some fighting is a normal and healthy part of growing up. The next chapter about brothers and sisters explores this in more detail, and is therefore of use even if you have only one child.

Using the process as a prompt

The mistakes process gives you a chance to reinforce all the skills you have learned in this book. For instance, you know that it doesn't help to go up the mountain of anger if your child is upset. It does help to prepare for success, to praise your child's positive behaviour and so on. But you are only human and sometimes, with the best will in the world, things just don't work out as intended. When everything has calmed down, that is the time to identify what didn't happen and admit the mistake – 'I lost my temper instead of keeping calm' or 'I forgot to remind you that we were not going to buy any treats at the shop today'.

Going through the mistakes process reminds you that there is always another chance to get things right next time!

CHAPTER 11

Taking the heat out of sibling rivalry

The relationship that your children have with each other may well be the longest relationship they have during their lives. Sibling relationships can be as important as the relationships between parent and child – most brothers and sisters spend a lot of time with each other when they are young and bond strongly with each other.

Siblings usually have mixed feelings towards each other. They can be a wonderful source of love, protection and never ending entertainment for each other. Yet at the same time they can be the source of jealousy, resentment and hurt.

If you have more than one child, you probably hope that your children will grow to have a close, loving relationship with each other. There is no guarantee that this will happen no matter how thoughtfully you bring them up – the many other influences on your children's relationships are totally out of your control. However, it is not unusual for adults who have difficult relationships with their siblings to trace their problems back to their childhood. They have not recovered from the jealousy and resentment that they felt for each other as children, rightly or wrongly believing that their parents preferred, or still prefer, one sibling over the other. You need to do your best to prevent this from being your children's experience – and that means paying particular attention to their relationships.

Most young siblings bicker and argue a lot. There can be many reasons for this. On an emotional level, many children compete for their parents' approval and love, believing there is not enough to go around. Each child wants to show you that he or she is stronger, smarter, more generous, sporty or helpful than their siblings so that, in their eyes, you will love them more. They also compete for your time and attention. The cartoon on page 36 shows a family that believes that they must compete with each other in order to get what they need. This is how most children experience the world.

At other times, the reasons for arguments are more prosaic – who can play with the blue truck and who is in charge of the remote control? Some fights are just games gone wrong. Others start when children are tired, hungry or unwell. And for lots of kids, winding up their brother or sister is an exciting pastime.

The ideas and skills described in this chapter address both the emotional and practical challenges of raising happy siblings. They will help you reduce unhealthy competition and jealousy, so that your children feel more warmth and less resentment towards each other. As a result, your own life will be calmer too.

Being fair

As your children grow up you can see that they have different talents, interests and opinions. Some children seem to crave more attention than others; some have a greater need for privacy. Some love new challenges and others stick to what they know in order to feel secure. Some are naturally tidy while others leave mess wherever they go. Some always have their nose in a book while others need people around them all the time.

It is difficult for parents not to make comparisons. 'Why can't he be like his brother?', or 'How come his younger sister is more organised than him?' we wonder in exasperation after the child in question lost his swimming trunks for the third time in one month. But the simple answer is that he cannot be like his brother because he is a different person therefore we need to treat him differently at times.

Children develop in different areas at different ages and with differing levels of ease. At certain points, one child may need more parental support than others. If you always try to treat your children equally, you are not being fair to them. To be truly fair, you need to give differently – to give to each child according to his or her individual needs.

The same principle applies with material possessions. For example, you may think: 'Laura needs new shoes. I'd better buy something for the others, otherwise they will be jealous.' Even though you have only the best of intentions when you do this, you may be digging yourselves into a hole. Trying to treat children equally in this way means constantly having to compare what you give them and, in doing so, you encourage your children to compare themselves to each other. Your children will be occupied with what their siblings are getting in order to make sure that they get their equal share. They will be on the alert for signs of not getting what they think they should, complaining and blaming when they think their siblings are favoured.

Giving children what they need

'It is the summer holiday and my two girls are staying with my family in Spain for a couple of weeks. They absolutely love it there, but one issue used to spoil our evenings until I sorted it out a few days ago. Whenever I rang them, the girls used to fight over the phone, trying to snatch it from each other, shouting and screaming. They'd make nasty comments about each other and interrupt each other's conversation. I could hear my poor mother in the background, pleading with them, to no avail, to calm down. None of us enjoyed the calls, and I sometimes even wished I could avoid them altogether.

'We tried to get the girls to take turns, but they refused. We also tried to give each one of them a fixed time on the phone so that the other could have a go after that, but they didn't want that either.

'I suddenly realised that they both felt that each moment I spent with their sibling came at their own expense. So I promised each one of them that they could talk to me for however long they wished, and that I would not hurry them, even if it was the middle of the night and I could hardly keep my eyes open. From the moment I made this promise, they both calmed down and the fighting stopped. There was no need for me to share my time equally between them – and, indeed, no point in it. Once they each felt that they were getting enough of my time, they stopped being competitive. I still ring every night, and to my surprise our unlimited daily phone calls take no longer than they did before.'

Amanda, mother of six- and thirteen-year-old girls

So, instead of giving to them equally, you can say:

'Each one of you will get everything you need. You are all lovely, but different people, so you need different things at different times.'

Or: 'Being fair is giving you what you each need; there is enough for everybody.'

Try to resist the temptation to hide information or lie to protect your children from disappointment if one has received something that the other hasn't. When parents do this, they are unintentionally setting siblings against each other: one has a secret that should not be told to the other.

For example, a parent says to the daughter: 'I'll get you some hot chocolate but don't tell your brother. He will be really upset that he didn't get one too.' This creates an unnecessary dilemma for the daughter. She wonders what she should do if her brother asks. She wonders if she should lie. And she wonders if there is anything secret that her brother is getting that she doesn't know about. Imagine what would happen if she does tell her brother about the hot chocolate, including the fact that the parent asked for it to be kept secret. The brother will feel betrayed by his sister and his parent.

Since you don't need to treat your children equally, you don't need to worry about giving them the same amount of hot chocolate! Each child will know that whenever they want something extra to eat or drink and it is appropriate for them to have something, they will be given it.

As long as you are able to say to each one of your children, 'If you needed that, I would give it to you as well,' you are being fair.

Bickering is inevitable

Children's never ending bickering and arguing can be very disheartening for parents. Not only do you wish that your children got on well with each other, you also want peace and quiet for yourselves, at least for some of the day. But you need to remember that a certain amount of arguing and fighting is completely healthy and normal. By arguing and fighting with each other your children learn to stand up for themselves, to share, to negotiate and to express themselves. Through play-fighting, they also learn about how to defend themselves physically. Fighting with siblings is a good preparation for thriving in the school playground. Not all of what appears to you to be inappropriate interaction between your children feels the same to them.

It is not realistic to expect children always to be happy in each other's company. If you try to control your children so that they are always kind to each other and never fight, you have very little chance of success. In the attempt, you will become more and more frustrated, and so will they.

Taking sides

In this instance, Mum wants to work out what happened between her two children but she does not stand much of a chance.

So, who is right here? The answer is that, usually, it is both and neither. Most fights start when one sibling does some small annoying thing; the other reacts to it, the first one does even more of what they were doing, the other reacts more strongly, and so on until a full-blown sibling war is taking place. This process is very similar to the mountain of anger depicted on page 77. Both siblings truly believe that they are in the right and that it is all the other's fault. As they are immature, they usually see only their own point of view, and do not even attempt to understand that of their sibling. Even if they know that they did something wrong, they will hate to admit it – they don't want their sibling to 'win'.

There is rarely a way for parents to find out who started a fight. Therefore it is usually a mistake to apportion blame according to what you see – there is a lot that happens between siblings that you do not know about. By taking one sibling's side you are in fact alienating the other, who is likely to become resentful and bitter, and determined to harm the sibling you wanted to protect. You may think that you are helping the child whose side you take but, in fact, you are creating problems for him or her – he or she now has an even angrier sibling to deal with. This resentment can fester for days or even years; you may soon forget all about the incident but the sibling that you blamed will probably remember.

Despite her best intentions, Mum's interference is unlikely to be helpful.

In many families, the younger sibling knows exactly what to do in order to push the older one's buttons. Parents frequently take the younger child's side, believing that the younger one needs to be protected and that the older one should know better. So the younger child learns to go on hurting the older sibling quite safely under parental protection. By supporting a child you are giving them your own power as a parent. The other child feels powerless, angry and resentful.

However, sometimes one child routinely hurts the other, even though unprovoked. If this is the case in your home, you can find out why this may be happening and what to do about it in the pages that follow.

Practical steps for raising happier siblings

These are the most important things parents can do to help their kids get on better with each other:

1 Spend time with each child individually.

2 Keep out of arguments and fights.

3 Help children create their own solutions to everyday disputes.

4 Give positive attention when children are not fighting with each other.

5 Allow your children to tell you what they feel about each other, even if you are not comfortable with what they say.

6 Take care of each child's individual needs.

If you want good results, do everything on the list.

1 Spend time with each child individually

When I work with parents, I often ask them to tell me about their ways of improving sibling relationships. They usually come up with lots of good ideas but rarely with this one, which is on the top of my list.

Because children need their parents' positive attention so much, they benefit a lot from having one parent all to themselves, even if just for a little while. And it is usually the child that you find more challenging who needs you the most. When your relationship with a child is going well, this child already feels secure and accepted and so is usually less desperate for your time, attention and approval. But a child whose behaviour is difficult for you to manage, or who has a very different set of interests from your own, may not feel a strong enough bond with you and therefore needs the extra time and attention even more.

If you feel that you do not have much in common with one of your children, say he is very much into football or computer games and you are completely uninterested, then it may be easier to let him spend a lot of time on his computer or with his other parent. Unfortunately, if you let this happen, you may find after a while that the two of you have drifted even further apart. It is well worth while finding something that you can enjoy doing together, or ask your child to explain to you about his interests and make an effort to get involved. Even if you are not interested in the topics that inspire him, you will get closer to your child and connect better with him. Spending this extra time can be especially helpful if you have been having problems with that child's behaviour. Having fun together can help you put the bad feeling behind and turn a new leaf.

Parents who start spending individual time with each one of their children report experiencing a new level of connection with them and say that their children talk to them about their lives at such times in a way they wouldn't otherwise do. They feel that they have rediscovered their children and are surprised to find how wonderful this can be. And most importantly, a child who has a chance to get undivided attention from each of his parents does not have such a strong urge to compete for it with siblings.

2 Keep out of arguments and fights

If you are used to getting involved whenever your children fight, they have probably learned already that fighting is an effective way to get your attention. Because parent attention is so important for children, they are likely to fight even more to get it.

Moreover, when you become the arbitrator and the judge in their fights, your children learn to come to you instead of resolving the matter themselves. And because they want to look good in your eyes, they may exaggerate their sibling's misdemeanours or even tell straight lies. What started as a little argument can become much worse when parents get involved.

You need to do two things in order to break this pattern. The first is to reduce your attention to fights while they happen, and the other (see Step 3) is to help children find solutions to their problems once they calm down. Let your children know in advance that you are not going to interfere unless the fight becomes dangerous, in which case you will separate them. Since you are not going to take sides anyway, there is not much point in finding out the details of what happened – this is just another form of giving your children attention for the wrong thing.

If you cannot stand the noise when your children are fighting, you could, perhaps, put music on or leave the room. If you are in the car, pull over until they calm down, and then wait another minute just to be absolutely sure that they have. Tell children in advance that this is what you are going to do, and explain that it is dangerous for you to drive when this bickering is going on.

Your help is very much needed but, for it to be effective, you need to give it when everybody is calm, not while the sibling wars are on. The next step describes how to give help effectively.

3 Help children create their own solutions

Arguments about belongings and sharing, TV viewing and computer use are normal in all families. A large proportion of children's squabbling is about these practical matters: Who can sit next to Daddy at dinner? Whose turn is it on the computer now? Is one child allowed to touch the other one's bed?

If you look deeper into these arguments, you can see that they concern the need to have a sense of control, attention, achievement or privacy. Developing a practical plan to resolve these issues will allow your children to relax, knowing that their needs and wishes are respected, even if they do not always get exactly what they want.

At a time when everyone is calm, raise one of the concerns that your children argue over and invite each one of them in turn to say how they would like things to be. Then ask your children for their ideas for resolving the issue in question. Say that you trust them to think of solutions, and praise them when they are willing to share or compromise. When you use children's ideas, they are much more likely to stick to the new agreements. And children often come up with solutions that are far more creative than those of their parents'!

If any of your children believe that they were treated unfairly, you may need to go through the mistakes process with them first (see Chapter 10). Children may need to admit their mistakes and make amends before they can move on. If you are worried that this conversation may deteriorate into a fight, you may want to talk to each of your children separately first.

Of course, when children are too young to think this way, the family management team will need to decide the rules. But in my work, I regularly see children who are capable of much more thinking than their parents give them credit for. Also, try asking your older child what may help him or her to have a better time with a younger sibling, and what will help him or her to like that younger sibling more. You may be surprised by the reply!

When you have all agreed a plan, treat it like a family rule – write it down and put it in a place where it can be seen by everyone. A part of the plan needs to address what will happen if children do not stick to the agreement so that you have something to fall back on when things do not go as planned. Here are some examples for family rules to help siblings get on better:

- Each child has 30 minutes each day on the computer, and must willingly relinquish it to their sibling if it is their turn when the 30 minutes are up. When a child refuses to leave the computer, the extra time is measured and taken off the next day's allotted time. You can get your children a timer and help them monitor it themselves.

- Personal equipment is private and cannot be borrowed without permission. You can mark the equipment if you are not sure who owns what. If one child breaks the rule, a good consequence could be for the offending child to do something small for the other to make up for it.

- When one of the children's friends comes over, that child has to let the other siblings join them for 15 minutes and then they may play with the friend without the siblings around. It is unrealistic to expect children to always include their siblings in the games when they have friends over.

4 Give positive attention

The more attention you give a particular behaviour, the more your children are likely to repeat it. So if you want your children to get on better with each other, give them a lot of positive attention whenever they are getting on well, even it is for just for a few seconds! The time when your children are not at each other's throats will stretch and stretch.

Here are some examples of things you can say:

- 'You let your sister play with your bricks. That was very kind.'

- 'Thanks for pouring milk for your brother as well as for yourself.'

- 'You didn't snatch anything from the baby. I really appreciate this.' (Say this before your child has had a chance to snatch. Don't wait for a whole day without any snatching.)

- 'You picked up the crayon that your brother threw on the floor – that was very helpful!'

- 'We got into the car today, and there were no arguments about where you were going to sit! You just got on with it, both of you!'

- If your children do argue in the car, you can say, 'You argued a bit about who would sit where, and you were able to come to a solution yourselves. I'm very proud of you two for sorting out your own issues!'

- And if they argued and could not resolve the concern, 'It was really difficult for you to sort out who would sit where, and I'm glad that you accepted what I said you should do. You realised that we had to leave and that only one of you could get what they wanted.'

Make sure each child gets some praise. Some children actually ask for praise when you praise their sibling – why not praise them too? It costs nothing!

5 Allow your children to tell you what they feel about each other

When one of your children comes to you complaining about a sibling, it is very tempting either to tell them to 'get on with it' or to try and figure out what happened and offer solutions. Instead, ask yourself why they are complaining.

Your child may be telling tales in order to get a sibling in trouble and to look good in comparison. For instance, one child may say that his sister helped herself to a biscuit from the cupboard or hasn't brushed her teeth. This creates a dilemma for you – if you act on this, your daughter may become extremely resentful, feeling that you are all ganging up on her. It will also encourage the child telling tales to continue doing so. On the other hand, if you do nothing it may look as if you are condoning your daughter's behaviour, giving the other siblings a licence to behave in the same way. Your best option is to explain to all your children that it is your responsibility, not theirs, to make sure that all children do the right thing and that you are not interested in their stories about each other unless they were personally hurt, or something dangerous or damaging is going on. If your children still tell tales, just repeat that you are not going to listen because it is not their job to police their brothers and sisters.

If your child is complaining that the sibling has caused some hurt, physically or emotionally, use reflective listening as explained in Chapter 7. Here are some examples:

Responses to valid complaints

Your child says:	Suggested responses:
Mike ruined my train track.	Oh, no! You worked really hard on it! Won't it be lovely when Mike grows up and realises he can't mess up your things?
Chloe pushed me out of her room and it really hurts.	You wish she would welcome you into her room and you could go there whenever you like.
	It probably feels unfair that you don't mind her going into your room but she doesn't like you going into hers.
I hate Anna.	You sound furious with her.
	Maybe you sometimes wish that we could return her to the hospital for a while until she can walk and talk and play with you.

It is very possible that both children will come to you with complaints about each other, in which case you can listen in the same way to both. When you allow your children to express their feelings, even when these feelings are uncomfortable for you, your children will feel accepted and understood. And they will be less likely to lash out and hurt their sibling. Of course, you can also help them find solutions to their problems (as in Step 3).

6 Take care of each child's individual needs

If you see that one of your children is constantly angry and starts fighting with siblings without apparent provocation, you might want to look a little further afield for an explanation. For example, many children who experience difficulties at school take their frustration out on their siblings at home. If this is the case, you will need to find out what is happening at school and raise any concerns there. Happy children do not regularly fight with their siblings when not provoked. And frustrated children will keep on resenting their siblings until their problems are resolved.

Some children, however, start fighting just because they need to let off steam. They may need plenty of opportunities for exercise and free play, and boys, especially, may need opportunities to play-fight. It is best if they can do that with their dad or with another male friend or relative. If they get enough opportunities to play-fight, they are likely to be less aggressive towards other people, including their siblings.

One of your children may have some highly annoying habit or behaviour, or is too boisterous, or is lacking in age-appropriate social skills. Although this child may not set out to annoy their siblings, they may get irritated nevertheless! You can help your child improve – simply take them aside and show them what they need to do differently. For instance, you can help them practise asking for something without whining or sharing a toy without

---

Practising solutions

'I make special efforts to walk with my twins Lily and Tim to school, even though I need to get to work and their nanny is already on hand. But our walks often used to turn to battlegrounds, for one reason or another. One morning I had to withdraw some money from the cashpoint. I asked Lily to type in the PIN number and Tim to put in the card, but they both wanted to take the cash! Lily grabbed it and Tim tried to snatch it from her, and they both ended up wailing and screaming all the way to school. That was the last straw. I could take it no longer.

'I knew that there was no point in discussing the detail of what happened, and that trying to arbitrate between them would lead me nowhere. I was also angry and resentful and knew I needed a break. So I told the children's teacher that they were fighting all the way to school, and that, for a week, they would come to school with their nanny, while we practised sorting out problems without fighting. The teacher explained to them that she completely understood me and that she hoped they would learn to get on better with each other soon. The children and I used the week to discuss together how they needed to behave and what they could do when things went wrong. I complimented both Lily and Tim during the week for their understanding and improving attitude.

'We started walking to school together again with great anticipation. I was quick to praise the children for their excellent behaviour and grown-up attitude, and kept saying how much I now enjoyed their company. Their teacher joined me in complimenting them and so did their father. They have been walking to school beautifully for the last three weeks, feeling proud of themselves and getting plenty of positive attention. I even suspect that they enjoy each other's company. I certainly do.'

Andrea, mother of six-year-old twins Lily and Tim

---

snatching, or agree on a sign you can give when they start tapping or making strange noises without being aware of it. It is best to do this when other siblings are not around, to avoid the risk that they might feel humiliated.

A new baby arrives

When a new baby is born, the whole identity of each sibling is challenged. The roles that they so carefully made for themselves – as your only child or your cutest younger child – are now being shaken. This is especially difficult for your first born who until now lived in a world of adults – now there is only some of your attention, time and care available. Tiny babies are new and exciting and everybody seems to take much more interest in them. They must be fed, carried and held in your arms for many hours, being physically close to you, while older siblings are pushed further away. Most older siblings will resent the new 'intruder' and feel jealous, cry, become clingy, sometimes hit the little one or sweetly suggest that you return it to where it came from.

On top of all this you are probably exhausted from the birth and the sleepless nights. You have this new little person to tend to and a demanding older child is not what you need. The adjustment to the new baby can last for many months. Some children who are quite happy when their younger sibling is born become resentful once the baby starts crawling around and snatching things. Luckily, there is a lot you can do to help your children accept the new baby. It will make life easier for all of you.

You can prepare in advance: explain about what babies are like, what they do and how they need to be cared for. Talk about how life changes when a new baby arrives and use reflective listening when your children express concerns. Read together one of the many good books designed for this purpose and perhaps take the older sibling to the ultrasound checks (if the hospital permits this) or to listen to the baby's heartbeat, so that he or she can see or hear that the baby is real!

If your children are close in age to each other, make sure that the older one gets used to his or her new bed months before the new baby is born, and make any other necessary changes well in advance, so that it does not feel as if the new baby has pushed the older children out of their territory. Teach your children to be as independent as possible so that they are less reliant on you and praise them for their new skills.

Before the baby is born, it can be useful to remind well-meaning friends and relatives to pay a lot of positive attention to the older siblings when they come to visit, and perhaps even give gifts to the older siblings instead of to the baby, who cannot appreciate them anyway.

Check which of the practical steps in this chapter can be helpful to you. Pay particular importance to spending time individually with older siblings when the baby is not around. This will meet some of their need for your time and attention and will help them relax more when the baby is there.

A quick recap

It is natural for kids to bicker and fight and it is unrealistic to expect them to always be kind to each other but we can help our children improve their relationships in many ways.

- Treat each child according to their individual needs rather than aiming to treat all children equally.

- Spend time with each child individually.

- Help children come up with solutions to their disputes while keeping out of squabbles when they happen.

- Give children a lot of positive attention, in particularly descriptive praise, when they get on well with each other.

- Listen to children's feelings about each other without taking sides.

- Take care of children's individual needs, so that they feel better in themselves and are less likely to take their frustration out on their siblings.

If you choose to take on the ideas above and follow the practical steps recommended you will be delighted to see your children resenting each other less and enjoying each other more. Each one of your children will feel accepted and respected for who they are, and will be less busy competing with his or her siblings. Your children will learn that there is no limit to your love and approval – there will always be enough for everybody.

CHAPTER 12

Time to play

When you think back to when you were a child, you can probably remember endless hours spent playing in nearby fields, parks or in the street with your friends, walking to places by yourself, climbing up trees, getting lost and found and in and out of trouble. Your parents probably didn't always know where you were and what you were up to, yet you survived! Having the freedom to learn from your mistakes, you slowly became more confident and more streetwise.

Children today have a very different experience of their free time. Very many are taken to and from school by adults, spend much of their time after school in organised activities, have their play closely monitored and spend many more hours in front of the TV and electronic games. And their parents are much more involved with everything that they do.

There are advantages to this shift – if your kids are around more you can play with them, teach them things and be closer to them. But having your kids nearby so much of the time can put a lot of pressure on you – you get little respite and your children stay dependent on you and less able to occupy themselves. And children of this generation have far less freedom and control over what they do with their time, which is difficult for them as well.

This chapter is about play – having fun with your children and helping them to enjoy playing by themselves or with friends. We will talk about free play, sport and board games, winning and losing, balancing safety and risk and, of course, ways to manage TV and electronic equipment wisely. Play is essential for kids. This is how they learn and develop. When they have a positive experience of their play time, and spend relaxing, fun time with you, their mood improves and so does their behaviour.

Playing with your kids

Young children do not distinguish between play and learning, or indeed between playing and being. They are endlessly curious and excited by their surroundings, constantly trying, testing and experimenting. They have a wonderful ability to enjoy the moment that we, as adults, often lose. They can help you rediscover the joy of watching a butterfly for five minutes, splashing in puddles endlessly or playing frisbee in the park. You can help your children learn and play just by doing things with them, allowing them some freedom to explore at their own pace and answering their questions. You will need to accept though, that anything you do is likely to take much longer than you are used to.

The following pages explain what children gain from different kind of games and how to get the most out of playing together. For ideas for particular games and activities, look at the Recommended reading list on pages 200–201.

Chores as games

Although you are unlikely to be excited about laundry or preparing meals, young children usually are. You can get children to load the washing machine and press the right buttons. They can help you sort out the clothes or just chat to you while you are busy. As long as you are positive with them they will be happy.

Kids of all ages can join you in the kitchen, having fun and doing jobs starting with mixing, pouring and weighing food ingredients to cracking eggs, making fun sandwiches and eventually cooking and even making whole meals. Allow the young ones to play with food or with ingredients: dough, dried pasta, rice, beans or dried lentils. Let them arrange finger foods on a plate or combine the ingredients to make a salad.

Involve them in what you are making and give them jobs that are actually helpful. When children are young and slow, try to think of tasks they can do that are not critical, and will not hold you up. You don't want to get stressed out when they still haven't finished peeling the one clove of garlic you must add to your frying pan right now.

As well as being fun, getting children into the kitchen is one of the best ways to encourage them to be flexible and adventurous with what they eat.

Board games

When you play board or card games with your kids, you are not just having fun! Your children also learn and practise new thinking and social skills. Younger children practise skills such as counting, adding up, recognising patterns, estimating, grouping things together and memorising. Older children learn planning, strategising and risk assessment. Children learn naturally as they play – there is no need to turn their games into mini-lessons. They also learn social skills: taking turns, being patient while allowing their playing partner to think, winning graciously and losing without being devastated. And of course, they get to practise following rules!

When a child becomes proficient in a particular game, this can contribute greatly to their sense of self-esteem. Games are as important as school work, so try to find some time to play with your children, even if this means that something else will need to give.

Sport

If you are sporty yourself, you are probably already making sure that your children spend time playing sport and being active. But if you are not into practising any sport, it may be worth remembering that children's most fundamental sense of confidence comes from being comfortable in their own body. Kids who are strong, healthy and well coordinated have an air of self-confidence that is usually evident to others. They are less prone to accidents and are less vulnerable to bullying.

In many schools, being good at football is almost a guarantee for having something to do in the long lunch break. It also ensures a higher social status, especially for boys, and helps in making friends. Girls (as well as some boys) who are into gymnastics love showing off their cartwheels and handstands. Swimming lessons are compulsory in school – competent swimmers have a great time while poor swimmers can feel utterly miserable. Whatever sport you choose together, on top of the obvious benefits your children will be practising some or all of these important life skills: giving their best, coping with physical discomfort and with disappointments, being honest, accepting decisions that they do not like and working in a team.

Do I let them win?

We've all battled with this dilemma. From the Snakes and Ladders years to playing draughts, rummy, table tennis or rugby with older children, parents ask themselves: Should we pretend that we are less competent than we are, or otherwise deliberately lose games so that we can let them win? Your kids may hate losing and if they lose too much, they may give up on playing with you altogether. You certainly don't want this to happen. You also want to build up your kids' confidence, so letting them win may seem like a good idea. But sooner or later, your kids may suspect that you have been doing this for a while, and they may feel cheated and have a crisis of self-confidence. In any case, it doesn't feel great to be less than honest with your kids. So what is the way out of this?

We first need to realise that having clumsy, hapless and half-witted parents is not at all reassuring for a child. You are the people providing for your children, keeping them safe and meeting many of their other needs. You are not of much use to them if you are still struggling with the basics, are you?

It's best to play with your children for real, while giving them a fair chance at winning. To achieve this you can impose a handicap on yourself, and then play full out. Start your draughts game with fewer pieces or make a rule that you have to play your move instantly, while your child is allowed to take time to think. Agree that to win your table-tennis match you will need 21 points while your child will only need 10. Explain to your child that this is only fair – you are older and more experienced so you need to work harder for your wins. As your children grow up you can reduce the handicap gradually and celebrate each step! They will see their progress and be happy with their success, and your game will become exciting and genuine, with a good balance between winning and losing. If you want your young children to have a better chance of winning Snakes and Ladders, even though it is based on luck not skill, let them start halfway on the board (this has the added benefit of shortening this particular game, which I doubt is very exciting for you).

What if they still hate losing?

This is very natural for little kids but unfortunately some children stay sore losers well into their teens! If you are worried about a sulk or a tantrum if your child loses, it is best to prepare for it in advance. Before you start playing, ask your children how they think they will feel if they win and if they lose. Ask if they think they are going to cry, or maybe they will be able to handle it? Then stop a few times during the game and ask the same questions again. This prompts children to reflect on their actions and feelings, and prepares them for a potential disappointment. Most children will reassure you that they can accept a loss with grace, and will be able to do so when it comes to the crunch. Remember to compliment your child for any improvement, even if their behaviour was not perfect: 'You understand that it's okay to lose some games – I'm really proud of you'.

Of course, it is always helpful to model gracious losing

yourself. You can say 'You win some and you lose some, and although I'd rather win, I am okay with losing too'. Tell your children stories about losing games as a child or an adult. Your children may not be happy about losing, but it is more likely that they will accept it.

Free play and downtime

It seems that most of us have very little free time. When we are not at work, we rush around running errands or trying to keep our children busy and forget that we all need some time for not doing much at all. Parents need to have time when they can read the paper or have a chat with a friend. Children want and need downtime too. Often, a large part of their weekday is spent in a nursery or school with lots of other children around, being required to conform and perform. It is good for them to have times when nothing is arranged and they needn't do anything at all.

Some amount of boredom is good for kids' imagination – it stimulates them to create activities to occupy themselves. You do not always need to play with your kids, to have their friends over or to get them to participate in extra-curricular activities. Sometimes you just need to keep them safe and enable them to explore and create. Not all time with children needs to be 'quality time'. Allow children time for free play and for reading, with you close at hand but busy doing other things. Sometimes all children need is to know that you are there, so that they can show you their latest creations or elaborate inventions.

To help them play creatively you can supply children with inexpensive materials and props: from the obvious paper, crayons, paint, glue, colourful pictures from magazines and scissors (make sure that they know how to use them safely first), to old clothes, scarves and hats for make-believe play, old pots and pans, wooden and plastic spoons, plastic cups and bowls for playing with water in the garden. The list goes on and on – old bedsheets, the inside of toilet rolls, kitchen foil, cereal boxes, avocado and apricot stones, buttons, shells, pieces of string or elastic bands... I'm sure you can come up with more ideas yourself.

It is best to rotate toys and props so that your children do not get overloaded and bored. And, needless to say, visit your local library and get some books. As soon as your children are old enough to venture out themselves, the library can be a good place for them to go to.

Independent play

Your children may love to play independently sometimes, without any adults around and without the aid of electronic games or TV. They may disappear for hours, making structures out of shoeboxes, playing pretend games with their doll's house, making a shelter for snails in the garden or just reading. If you have more than one child, your kids may be able to keep each other entertained with only the occasional inevitable fight. If this is how things are at your home, congratulate yourself and feel free to skip the rest of this section.

However, if your children are reluctant to play on their own without electronic aids, or to let you have a short break when you need one, then you need to help them learn to enjoy independent play. As with teaching everything new, it is best to start gradually:

- Tell them you are going to read the paper for one or two minutes and they must play quietly by your side. Or say that you need to complete a specific, well-defined task (such as peeling a few potatoes) before you are going to respond to them. As they get better at occupying themselves, make these time intervals longer and longer.

- Let them stay in the room with you as long as they don't disturb you.

- Give them a mirror activity. If you are reading the paper, give them an old paper to draw on or cut up, or if you are cleaning the kitchen, get them a not-too-wet mop so that they can 'clean' too.

- Suggest they play with something that you know engages their concentration or imagination, or give them a challenge such as a puzzle, promising to have a look once their independent playing time is over.

- Gradually get them to move into another room. Start with as little as two seconds if this is a problem for your child.

- Always stick to your promised finish time so they know they can rely on your word. Setting a kitchen timer together with your children can be very helpful. They will learn about time and your mind will be free to concentrate on your chosen activity rather than being occupied with how long you still have. Alternatively, you can point to a number on the clock and tell your kids they can come and find you when the big hand points to that number.

- Praise them descriptively for any new step that you want to encourage – going to another room in the house, staying there for a slightly longer time, playing out in the garden by themselves etc.

If your kids created something by themselves, ask to see it and be generous with your enthusiasm and descriptive praise. Describe what you like about what they made, give them a big hug and a compliment for being independent and grown up. If you used this time to rest or to get on with your chores, your children would enjoy hearing how helpful they were playing on their own. For instance, you can give a hug and say 'Thank you so much for letting me have these five minutes. This email was constantly on my mind, and now that I've sent it off, I can stop thinking about it and give all my attention to you. I'd love to see what you made. Will you show me?'

Time with individual children

Not all fun activities need to involve the whole family. Children love having one parent all to themselves, even if you are only going to walk the dog. They can get plenty of attention and affection without worrying about anyone else getting in the way. This was already discussed in the Chapter 11 covering siblings.

Even if you have only one child it is good for everybody if the child spends some time alone with each parent. This will give one of you a chance to have uninterrupted quality time with your child, while allowing the other some much-deserved child-free time. It also means you can focus on things you particularly like doing. For example, you may love to read books with your child while your partner is happier kicking a football round the garden. It makes sense for each of you to do what you are best at, as long as you both stay involved.

Family outings

We all love going out and doing things with our children from time to time. Yet we can end up with a feeling of irritation and failure if the carefully planned outings to swimming pools and museums end with children complaining about the journey, refusing to eat the food prepared or demanding toys and sweets. We sometimes feel it would have been better not to have set off at all.

You can prevent all this by involving your children in the planning and preparation for the outing. If you are preparing a picnic, get your children to help – they are more likely to eat it if they took part in making it. Give your children some limited choice as to where you are going, if this is at all practical. They will feel more involved and want the plan to succeed.

When going to a familiar place, ask your kids what they think will happen and how they need to behave. If you are going somewhere new, give them some information while explaining that there are some things you are not sure about, and that you all need to be a bit flexible and trust that everything will work out. It is all a big adventure! Then compliment your children for every little thing that they do well.

When you go out as a family, simple pleasures are usually the best. Exploring parks a bit further away from your home, cycling together or feeding the ducks on the local pond are all highly enjoyable activities for children. When you make simple plans, you will feel much more relaxed about changing them as you go along.

It is easy to forget just how slow young children can be – it sometimes feels as if they live in a different time zone. There will always be someone needing to go to the toilet at the last minute or urgently needing to find a particular toy or protesting that they are hungry two minutes after leaving home. It is not a military manoeuvre, it is a fun outing – relax and keep it flexible. And remember, it does not matter if you do not manage to complete all your plans. The important thing is to enjoy your time together.

Label your special time

When you play with your children or take them out to do something together, tell them that this is your special time and let them know that you enjoy being with them. Sometimes children take their parents for granted and do not even realise that they are making an effort to spend time with them. When you label time with your children as their special time, and explain that you chose to be with them instead of doing other things that you like, they will appreciate being with you even more. The same amount of effort will have a much bigger positive impact on your children.

Special shopping time

'My son used to be uninterested when I suggested that he come with me to the shops on Saturday morning. He completely changed his attitude when I told him that this will be our special time together and that we could talk about whatever he liked. He now can't wait to go.'

John, father of eight-year-old Alex

If your schedule is hectic and it is difficult for you to commit to spending time with your children on a predictable basis, it is best not to promise things in advance but instead make your special time together a surprise. When you know, last minute, that you are going to have the time, decide on something special, such as a pillow fight or an extra-long bedtime story with your child, and tell your child to get prepared! (Agree this first with your partner, if you have one.) This way, your short time with your child will have a much bigger impact. If you have more than one child, spend time with each of them like this, whenever you can. Your children will enjoy the anticipation as well as their time with you. And they may have fond memories of these magic times years later.

TV, computer games and the internet

TV, computers and the internet are an accepted part of most people's lives. They do, however, need to be managed wisely. They enrich our children's world by exposing them to experiences that they would not otherwise have. There are wonderful nature and history programmes on TV, and other educational and entertaining programmes for kids or for families to watch together. Some computer games require children to use their bodies, improving their coordination and stamina. The internet is invaluable for homework and research, and is great for chatting with friends, getting in touch with people from all across the globe, playing games and following various interests. There is no doubt that mastering the new technology is an essential life skill and it is wonderful to see your children acquire it effortlessly. Having children engaged with something electronic also frees you up to do other things while knowing that your children are safe and that they are not making too much mess.

However, more and more research is showing that spending too much time sitting in front of various screens can increase the chances of obesity and damage children's posture, attention span, and academic and social skills. Young children do not always understand what they see on TV – they cannot tell the difference between programmes and commercials, do not understand irony and can be disturbed by what they see on the news. Many TV programmes expose them to bad language and to a dubious moral code.

The internet is no better, with its inappropriate sites on which children may see images of people engaging in extreme violence or sex. And, of course, there are people out there who may intend them harm.

Furthermore, electronic entertainment often splits the family – each family member may end up in a different room in front of a different screen, absorbed in his or her own virtual world and hardly interacting with anyone else. Many adults and children eat in front of the TV, or else the TV is constantly playing in the background, drawing people's attention and making conversation irrelevant. You can read more about this in Sue Palmer's book (see Recommended reading on page 200).

Children need plenty of time to play without electronic equipment. When they read or play, they develop their own imagination and creativity. When they watch TV, they become passive consumers of other people's imagination and creativity. Time in front of the TV reduces the opportunity to develop social skills such as sharing, taking turns and negotiating. It also reduces the time available for physical activity, which they need not just for their health but also to improve their coordination and dexterity. If your children can find nothing to do unless some gadget is turned on, then that should be a cause for concern. You may need to support them in rediscovering and developing their ability to play by themselves or with others.

Control the gadgets

It is essential that you control the gadgets, rather than letting them control you. Experts agree that under-twos should not watch any screens, including TV, as this harms their developing brain. Opinions vary about the recommended limit for older children, but almost all agree that it should never be more than 90 minutes per day, and preferably much less.

Young children should only be able to access websites that you have approved, by using appropriate software controls. You can find out more about keeping children safe online by visiting the recommended website on page 202.

The best way to reduce the amount of time children spend in front of various screens is to have a family rule allowing children access to them for a limited time, and only after they complete all other required activities such as helping a bit in the house, doing homework and practising any instruments. If you can make sure that at least on some days of the week your children go to the park or participate in an after-school activity, there will be little time left for TV and electronic games during the week

By all means, allow your children to watch moderate amounts of age-appropriate TV programmes, watch carefully chosen films or to play appropriate computer games. A complete ban, as some parents try to impose, usually results in children begging to watch TV whenever they are out of their parents' sight. They may feel left out socially, as their friends will talk about programmes that they have never watched.

One useful idea is to make watching TV a family activity – plan your viewing together, sit and watch with your children and discuss what you saw, to help them develop a critical approach to what they watch, including the adverts that are trying to sell them things. Even if they watch on their own, encourage them to talk to you about what they have seen.

It is also a good idea to encourage your children to talk with you about the sites they visit online and the computer games they play. You will almost certainly be able to use the opportunity to learn some computer skills from them! Most children will be eager to share what they do with anyone who expresses an interest. Older children will almost always share at least some of what they do online if you are around and express genuine curiosity. You can also use this as a constructive way of monitoring that your security and safety controls are appropriate. As the children grow up, for example, seeing a friend has put personal information or a party invitation on a social networking site would be a good opportunity to discuss the risks of such sites without confrontation.

Keep screens in a public place

Many children have TVs or computers in their rooms from a young age. The advantages to the parents are clear – by giving each child their own equipment you avoid arguments and fights about what programme to watch and whose turn it is on the computer. You also get a free electronic babysitter – while your children are entertained by their screens you can go about doing the things you need to do.

But by allowing electronics into children's rooms, especially TV and computers connected to the internet, you lose control over what they watch and for how long, and with whom they interact online. Children can easily switch on their TV or computer without your knowledge and watch or do whatever they want. It is very tempting for children to hide their latest games under the duvet and play them after bedtime, or to switch on the TV when they wake up in the middle of the night. Sooner or later, your children will close the bedroom door and you will have no idea what is going on behind it.

It is far better to have all computers and electronic games in an area of your home that everyone uses, such as the kitchen or the living room, so that adults can always look over the children's shoulders and see what they are up to. You will be able to spot bad content and have a look at the sites that your children visit. This does not provide absolute protection, but it shows your children that you are monitoring them and that you care. One of the first questions that people who target vulnerable children online ask is, 'Where is your computer and can any adult see what you are doing?'

If several children have to share one computer, this will create a natural limit on the time they can spend online. The same goes for the TV – only one in the home will almost guarantee that you know what your children are watching.

Screens out of children's rooms

If your children already have electronic gadgets in their rooms, get together with your partner, if you have one, and plan together what you would like to do about it.

Some parents decide to move the electronics into an area in their home that is public, and create new family rules about sharing their use. Other parents decide to remove some of the electronics completely from the home until they feel in charge again. If your children turn the electronic equipment on in front of you, even when they know that they are not allowed to do this, removing some of the electronic equipment from the home temporarily may be the easiest way to get back in charge. Parents are usually apprehensive about doing this but often they find it much easier than they had anticipated. If you decide to take this step, make sure that this is not presented to your children as a punishment but as a positive step towards having a healthier lifestyle for all the family. Be available to guide your children through this transition – you may need to play with them and start them off with new activities until they learn to entertain themselves. Usually, after the initial moaning and complaining, children get used to the idea and find other things to do with their time.

After-school activities

Participating in some organised activities after school can be wonderful for most children. It gives them a chance to sample a variety of pursuits, as well as to develop their talents in areas that are not on offer at their school. On top of enjoying their chosen activity, children also get opportunities to make new friends with kids who share their interests. Even popular kids sometimes experience difficult social times at school. Being able to mix with other children elsewhere can help them get through this patch. Almost all kids will enjoy some after-school activities, but these can be especially beneficial in the situations described below:

- Children who struggle with schoolwork, perhaps due to a learning difficulty, can often excel in sport, art or drama. Being successful at something, whatever it is, can give a huge boost to their self-confidence. They will also get a chance to make new friends who are not aware of their academic difficulties.

- Highly academic children who are bored with the school curriculum can channel their mental powers into other pursuits such as chess, music or foreign languages.

- Children who are shy or not particularly popular at school can have an opportunity to make friends in new surroundings. They can especially benefit from training in the performing arts, in particular, drama.

- Kids whose coordination is poor or who are not very strong physically can benefit from non-team sports activities, in particular from training in martial arts. These kids often tend to be bullied – martial arts can help them develop confidence in their body and present themselves more assertively in the school playground. However, you need to make sure that they enrol in a class that is suitable for their level of ability.

There can certainly be too much of a good thing as far as after-school activities are concerned. If the activity is becoming yet another chore, you are probably doing too much. Children's most valuable learning comes from free play, and there is no need to overload them with other activities if they do not enjoy them. You can read more about this topic in Cassandra Jardine's book (see page 200).

Playing with friends

All children have a strong need to belong, not just to their family but also to their peer group. Making and keeping friends is a big part of this. Some kids are very popular while others have fewer friends. Some children, especially girls, tend to develop very close friendships where secrets are shared and loyalties are strong – and these sometimes get broken. Other children have looser contacts with other children who enjoy the same type of activities, such as sport or music. No one style of friendship is superior to the other. As long as your child has at least one good friend, there is nothing to worry about.

Not having any friends over more than a few weeks may need a closer look. Use reflective listening to help you understand what is happening. Try to see your child objectively. Is there anything about your child's behaviour that stands in the way of developing friendships? You may wish to consider whether they need to improve their social and friendship skills, and use the positive skills in the book to help you with this.

Most kids do not play outdoors on their own these days, so we need to help them develop their friendships by inviting their friends over. This is even more important if your child is having social difficulties at school. Having a school friend over will help them build the relationship with this child, who is likely to be kinder to them at school in the future. Having a friend from another school will provide reassurance that they are capable of friendship and that they can be liked by other children.

If your child is usually easy-going with friends and problems are rare, you need not worry. The children will probably disappear to another room or to the garden and you may not hear from them again until they are hungry! However, if friends' visits were challenging before, discuss the issue with your child and come up with solutions before the next time a friend comes around. Here are some of the most common challenges:

Your children find sharing difficult

We tend to expect our children to share all their toys and belonging with their friends, as well as to invite them into their bedrooms. But do our own friends share our wardrobe, books and music? Do they jump on our bed? Very unlikely. Ask your children what belongings they would like to keep private, and put them away before any visitors come over. This will allow your children to share their other belongings willingly and generously.

Children argue or fight

Arguments that look terrible to us are not necessarily so to our children. Some fighting is inevitable – this is how children learn to assert themselves, share, negotiate and compromise. It is best to keep out of the squabbles as much as is reasonably possible, and let the children sort things out. If things get too bad, you can separate the kids until they calm down. You can then help them find solutions, in the same way that you help siblings. A fractious visit from a friend is not necessarily a failure. It is a part of everyone's learning, and children are usually quick to forgive and forget.

Asking for special privileges.

Your children, or their friends, may ask for something that is not in line with your family rules (such as sweets or watching TV). It is best to talk to your children in advance about what is and isn't allowed – you may wish to make special concessions when friends are around but you certainly don't have to. Ask your children whether they would like to explain your family rules to their friends or whether they would rather you do it. Friends usually accept rules very easily – the hosting children are usually the problem.

Their siblings are in the way

Agree a family rule about friends – perhaps that the other siblings can be included for a short time, then leave the guest and the hosting child on their own. All this needs to be agreed in advance.

Managing risk

Do you remember the discussion on pages 17–18, where we talked about how we react to the world according to the way we interpret what is happening, not just according to reality? The way our attitude to risk as a society has changed in the last few decades is a good demonstration of this principle.

Statistics show that there has been no increase in the number of children abducted by strangers over the past 50 years, and that the risk for injury at home is far greater than outdoors. In most areas, street crime is very low. Yet we now worry about letting a ten-year-old child get a loaf from the corner shop, and we restrict kids' independent outdoors play more and more.

Much of this change is probably a response to media coverage. The few isolated incidents of children being kidnapped by strangers are given such an extensive exposure that we all become fearful. As this information is hammered into our consciousness day after day, we perceive this tiny risk as much greater. We worry that something bad may happen to our child, and also that we will be blamed for it. It will all be our fault.

Children's playgrounds have been made safer, with rubber surfaces and round corners and sea-saws that do not touch the ground. But there has been no reduction in injuries. This is

I watched him climb

'When I was a child, my mother was very anxious about my sister and me doing anything physically risky. For instance, we were strictly forbidden to ride bikes or climb trees, and that made me feel very left out when with other children. When I had my own children, I didn't want to be so restrictive. So I decided, within reason, to trust their own instinctive sense of keeping safe.

'My older son, Ben, was extremely confident in his body. From an early age he found that he could shin effortlessly up lampposts and loved doing so. By the time he was seven, he was shinning up a pretty high lamppost right outside his school. A part of me wanted to say, "Be careful! Don't fall!" but I kept my mouth shut and just watched him. I would get horrified looks from other mothers and I knew they were thinking that I was a reckless parent – often they told me I ought to stop him. But, although I felt uncomfortable, I stood my ground and let Ben climb. I trusted him to know how far he could go, and I'm glad I did. He never took silly risks and today, as a teenager, he is extremely athletic. He is also an extremely skilled footballer, relying on technique rather than brawn (he is very slim), and his agility and confidence have so far kept him safe from serious football injuries. It actually serves as a survival skill as well, so allowing him to do something "risky" when he was young has actually helped him develop the skills to keep safe.'

Leah, mother of two teenage boys

because children tend to take more risks – when they are going to be landing on a soft surface they tend to jump from higher up.

Risk and adventure is an inevitable part of children's lives. There is no completely safe way to raise children, and bad accidents do happen to good children who have good parents. Making a considered choice to allow your children to take risks because you believe this is what they need is not irresponsible or neglectful. In fact, it can feel much more difficult to let children take that risk than to stop them. And raising couch potatoes carries its own mental, social and medical risks.

Of course, if you believe that your children are particularly reckless, you can stop them and teach them to become more responsible. But for most kids, the best we can do is to let them play outdoors, watch from a distance and trust that they are as safe as they can be. And when they are ready, we can train them to cross roads, give them some sensible advice about safety and let them gradually discover the big wide world.

CHAPTER 13

Before we end...

I hope you have found the ideas and skills described in this book useful and that you are ready to put them into practice at home. But first, a health warning! When learning new skills and gaining new insights, it is natural to develop unrealistic expectations. You may imagine yourself always being understanding, never shouting, always praising, preparing for everything, never being lost for words – in short, being perfect!

This, of course, does not happen in the real world. We do our best, sometimes in difficult circumstances. We all have our good days and other days when we are not at our best. It is perfectly normal not to be on top of things at all times. A shout or a harsh word is nothing to fret about and does not damage our children if it is a relatively rare occurrence in an otherwise positive atmosphere and loving home. It does not make us failures; it makes us human. And humans need to be kind to themselves and reach out to others for help and support.

Imagine that your children have an emotional bank account.* You make deposits into that account by using all the skills in this book – positive communication, spending fun time together, helping children deal with their emotions, looking jointly for solutions, and avoiding criticism and blame. On the other hand, shouting, criticising or not being mindful enough of children's needs withdraws from their account.

Very Scientific Diagram #19c:
"Emotional Bank Account"

Praise, Hugs   Shouts, Criticism

* The 'emotional bank account' metaphor comes from Stephen R. Covey (see Recommended reading, page 200).

Children feel secure and happy when their emotional bank account has a healthy balance. Parents can achieve this by depositing into their bank account whenever possible. If your children's bank account is full and then you have a bad day and shout a bit, they will still be in credit. However, if the same happens when the account is nearly empty, the account will be overdrawn – your children will feel more miserable and will take longer to recover.

To be able to take good care of your children and deposit generously into their emotional bank account, you have to have something in your own emotional bank account. If you are overdrawn because you neglect to take care of yourself, you will have nothing to spare. So everyone's needs always have to be considered, and a balance achieved over time.

Taking on the ideas and the skills in this book require a special kind of effort – the willingness to take stock and try to understand your children's perspective, and constantly to be looking for ways to change what you do in order to make things better. It isn't always easy and it takes determination, but the payoff is huge. A calmer, more loving atmosphere at home and a lot more fun for all!

A healthy lifestyle

One of the most important steps that parents can take to improve children's behaviour, mood and wellbeing is to make sure that they eat healthily, exercise, spend enough time outdoors and sleep well. Here are the basics. (See also Recommended reading, pages 200–201.)

Nutrition

We now know that there is a strong link between children's health, behaviour and what they eat. Spirited children often calm down once their diet improves. Most parents do not know how good things can be until they take steps to make sure that their children eat what is right for them. Here are the principles of good nutrition. I'm sure that not all this information is new to you – have a look and see if some of it is:

- Go lightly on sugar and refined carbohydrates in soft drinks, biscuits, cakes, white bread and pasta. They create a surge of glucose in the blood, which operates on the brain a bit like a drug. Shortly after consuming these foods, some children become restless or hyperactive, and then lose concentration and energy, craving their next fix. Try to reduce these foods as much as you can, or combine small amounts of them with whole foods such as fruit and vegetables, wholemeal bread or rice and proteins, which are slower to digest.

- Avoid food colourings and other food additives as much as possible. They are chemicals without nutritional value and research has shown that some children respond to them in unhealthy ways, such as becoming hyperactive. It is better for your children to eat raw or homemade food or healthier prepared food if this is not practical.

- See that your child does not eat too much salt – most people in the UK eat 50 per cent more salt than is good for them. Except for the obvious crisps and salted nuts, many breads, biscuits, cheeses and ready-meals contain high levels of salt (also called sodium). Current NHS advice states that 0.6g of sodium to 100g of food is a lot.

- Make sure your children are getting enough quality protein from fish, eggs, nuts and pulses. In particular, your children need omega 3 fats. You can get these as supplements if you are not sure your children are getting enough from foods.

- Avoid trans-fats (hydrogenated or partially hydrogenated fats) in processed foods as far as possible – research shows that they have various undesirable effects. Read the labels of the food you buy if you are not sure.

- Beware of caffeine in cola, chocolate, energy drinks, tea and, of course, coffee. It acts as a stimulant on children and also suppresses their appetites.

- Some children are allergic or sensitive to particular foods, or may have deficiencies in vitamins or minerals. If you suspect this could be the case with your child, consult your GP or a nutritionist.

A varied diet including a lot of fresh fruit and vegetables and home-cooked food is best. Unfortunately, this is not easy to achieve given a hectic lifestyle and the plethora of prepared food that is available.

Of course, children love things that are not good for them. Don't we all? The secret is to make the offending foods less available gradually, rather than completely ban them. There is nothing as tempting as forbidden fruit. Buy and offer these foods occasionally in small quantities – do not store them around the house. It can be very difficult for children to resist temptation if they know that the food they crave is hiding in one of the cupboards.

Another unfortunate truth: if you want your children to develop healthier eating habits, the whole family's diet needs to change. It is unrealistic and inconsiderate to expect your child to choose a healthy option if you choose an unhealthy one yourself.

Exercise, fresh air and daylight

Children are a bit like puppies – they need to exercise every day. They react to a lack of exercise according to their temperament: some become boisterous and restless – they run around, jump on beds and sofas, knock things over, or become fidgety, impatient and demanding. Others become lethargic, bored and indifferent. They may switch on the computer or the TV as soon as they have a chance, and sit passively in front of the screen for hours.

Until not so long ago, perhaps even during your own childhood, children used to walk to school and play outdoors freely. Every day, they had a chance to exercise their bodies before being required to do any mental work. They got much more daylight, benefiting both physiologically and psychologically. Go back a hundred years, and most children were doing something physical for most of the day. Although our culture has changed a lot since then, our biology has not.

As well as calming children down, exercise helps develop their muscles and coordination. Children who use their bodies a lot become healthier, stronger and more confident. Without exercise, there is greater risk of obesity and illness, both in childhood and later in life.

The best way to get kids moving is to incorporate some exercise into their daily routine. Walk to school and back if you can. If school is too far away, get off the bus a few stops ahead or park your car further away and walk. Alternatively, if your children run around or play ball games in the school playground, get them there earlier. This is as important as academic work.

Children learn what is important by copying adults, so it is a good idea to find some activity that you can do together. Children absolutely love going cycling or hiking with their parents, or just running around chasing a ball in the park. Exercise is good for parents too!

Many parents worry about spending time outdoors during the winter. Children usually do not mind about the weather as long as they are appropriately dressed. There is excitement and adventure in walking in the rain or in strong wind, and a sense of achievement in overcoming the odds.

When it is impossible to spend time outdoors, after-school activities such as swimming, trampolining, dancing or martial arts are the next best thing. Electronic games requiring children to use their bodies, for example by playing virtual sports or dancing to music, can be good too.

Sleep

Do your children wake up easily in the morning? If not, they are probably not getting enough sleep. Sleep is essential for children's physical and mental wellbeing, and tired children can become miserable, lacking in concentration and very difficult to handle. Children differ in the number of hours that they need to sleep each night, but needing to drag them out of bed in the morning is a sure sign that they are not sleeping as much as they need to.

Of course, when you say to a child 'It's late now, you look tired, time to go to bed,' the typical response is rarely 'Thank you, Mummy, for reminding me, I must go to sleep immediately.' Children don't usually like to think that they are tired. Sometimes they don't even know that they are – they feel uncomfortable but have no idea why. At other times, children realise that they need to sleep but don't want to leave their parents and miss all the fun that they believe is happening when they are in bed. This is even more understandable if you are working long hours and your children feel that they are not spending enough time with you. Staying by themselves in a dark room, sometimes on another floor, is not tempting at all.

Expecting a child to sleep on his or her own is a recent historical development. In many countries whole families sleep together, or parents sleep separately while their children share a room. Sleeping with another living being gives young children a sense of belonging. If children do not like sleeping on their own they may be happier with a sibling or even with a pet in their room. Some parents do not mind young children sleeping with them while others hate it, and experts have different opinions about what is the best thing to do.

If your children find it difficult to sleep by themselves, remember that you are asking them to do something which is unnatural for them, and therefore you will need to put time and effort into making it happen. A calm bedtime routine, including a bath, brushing their teeth, a bedtime story, perhaps some descriptive praise, a hug and kiss help children ease themselves into sleeping. See that their bed is comfortable and that the room is inviting. Leaving the bedroom door slightly open or having a nightlight may help too.

If you are struggling with sleep issues, see page 201 for further recommended reading.

Recommended reading

Parenting skills and practical advice

Covey, Stephen R., *The 7 Habits of Highly Effective Families*, Simon & Schuster Ltd, New Ed edition, 4 Jan 1999

Faber, Adele and Mazlish, Elaine, *How to Talk So Kids Will Listen and Listen So Kids Will Talk*, Piccadilly Press Ltd, New Ed edition, 3 May 2001

Jardine, Cassandra, *How to Be a Better Parent: No Matter How Badly Your Children Behave or How Busy You Are*, Vermillion, 2003

Palmer, Sue, *Detoxing Childhood: What Parents Need to Know to Raise Happy, Successful Children*, Orion, 2007

Parker, Jan and Stimpson, Jan, *Raising Happy Children: What Every Child Needs Their Parents to Know – From 0 to 11 Years*, Hodder and Staughton, revised 2004

Sheedy Kurcinka, Mary, *Raising your Spirited Child: A Guide for Parents Whose Child Is More Intense, Sensitive, Perceptive, Persistent and Energetic*, Harper Perennial, Reprint edition, Sep 1992

After-school activities

Jardine, Cassandra, *Positive not Pushy: How to Make the Most of Your Child's Potential*, Vermilion 2005

Brothers and sisters

Parker, Jan and Stimpson, Jan, *Sibling Rivalry, Sibling Love: What Every Brother and Sister Needs their Parents to Know*, Hodder & Stoughton, 2002

Helping your children to develop a more positive outlook on life

Seligman, Martin E P, *The Optimistic Child: A Proven Program to Safeguard Children Against Depression and Build Lifelong Resilience*, Us Imports, Reprint edition, 17 Sep 2007

How to avoid overreacting to your children's behaviour

Harris, Bonnie, *When Your Kids Push Your Buttons And What You Can You Do About It*, Piatkus, 2003

The Human Givens approach

The Human Givens approach describes our basic emotional needs as the 'givens' of human nature, along with innate resources, such as memory, emotion, imagination, that we all have to help us meet these needs. Helping people fulfil their needs and make best use of their innate resources is at the heart of the Human Givens approach to wellbeing. The following books, all by Joe Griffin and Ivan Tyrrell, and published by HG Publishing, introduce the approach and detail how it can be used to help with anger, depression, anxiety or addiction.

Freedom from Addiction: The Secret Behind Successful Addiction Busting, 2005

How to Lift Depression … Fast, 2004

How to Master Anxiety: All You Need to Know to Overcome Stress, Panic Attacks, Trauma, Phobias, Obsessions and More, 2006

Release from Anger: Practical Help for Controlling Unreasonable Rage, 2008

Ideas for fun activities for the whole family

Iggulden, Conn and Iggulden, Hal, *The Dangerous Book for Boys*, HarperCollins, 2006

Musselwhite, Debbie, *Teach Yourself Things to Do as a Family*, Hodder Education, 2008

Nutritional advice for children

Blythman, Joanna, *The Food Our Children Eat: how to get children to like good food*, Fourth Estate, New Ed edition, 17 Aug 2000

Holford, Patrick and Colson, Deborah, *Optimum Nutrition for your Child's Mind*, Piatkus Books, 2006

School and academic work

Janis-Norton, Noel, *Could Do Better: How Parents Can Help Their Children Succeed at School*, Barrington Stoke, 2005

Single parenting

Ellis, Carolyn B., *The 7 Pitfalls of Single Parenting: What to Avoid to Help Your Children Thrive After Divorce*, iUniverse, 2007

Sleep problems

Byron, Tanya and Baveystock, Sacha, *Little Angels: The Essential Guide to Transforming Your Family Life and Having More Time with Your Children*, BBC Active, 2005

Useful resources

Parenting skills CDs and DVDs

A set of five audio CDs and two DVDs explaining and demonstrating the core 'Calmer, Easier, Happier' parenting skills. Recorded by Noël Janis-Norton. Available from The New Learning Centre (020 7794 0321, www.tnlc.info).

Websites for parents

There are so many online sources of information and advice, it is often bewildering. Here is just a selection of those I found during the course of my research, which I thought likely to be the most helpful.

www.bbc.co.uk/parenting
A wealth of information for parents and families, covering many aspects of family life such as child development, ideas for games, family finance, childcare and work-life balance.

www.bdadyslexia.org.uk
British Dyslexia Association offers information, resources and training about dyslexia in children and adults. If your child is finding schoolwork challenging, this is a good place to start exploring.

www.enjoyourchildren.com
My own website, dedicated to providing parents with the insight, knowledge and skill to have a great family life.

www.gameskidsplay.net
Plenty of ideas for games both indoors and outdoors, with clear and simple instructions.

www.kidscape.org.uk
Good information about bullying and safety. As well as information for parents, the site contains a section with information for kids.

www.kidsmart.org.uk
Information about keeping children safe while using mobile phones and the internet. Contains a section with information for children.

www.mumsnet.com
An excellent source of information and support. Includes an active discussion forum for parents, covering all aspects of parenting, child development and relationships. You can post your parenting questions and get advice from other mums. You can also ask to get in touch with local mums.

www.oneparentfamilies.org.uk
Up-to-date information about issues concerning lone parents such as benefits, housing, education, legal rights, etc. You can also obtain information by ringing their helpline. It is not a counselling service, but can direct you to services available in your area.
0800 018 5026

Telephone helpline

www.parentlineplus.org.uk
Offers a free, confidential, non-judgmental 24/7 telephone helpline. The calls are answered by parent volunteers who are trained to help parents find their own solutions to family problems.
0808 800 2222

Parenting courses

Parenting courses in the UK vary in quality, price and length. If you would like to attend a course, find out what is available in your area from your GP practice, your child's school, your health visitor, your library or local parents. Currently there is no comprehensive central register of parenting courses, and your GP clinic or health visitor may not always know what is available, so do not give up!

Parenting UK
For a list of parenting courses throughout the UK (this list is not comprehensive).
www.parentinguk.org/3/for-parents

The New Learning Centre
Offers excellent courses in London and other UK locations.
211 Sumatra Road, London NW6 1PF
020 7794 0321
www.tnlc.info

The Parent Practice
Runs similar courses in South London.
68 Thurleigh Road, London SW12 8UD
020 8673 3444
www.theparentpractice.com

Index